SHARPEN Y IN

*P*ROJECT

MANAGEMENT

SHARPEN YOUR TEAM'S SKILLS IN

*P*ROJECT

MANAGEMENT

Jean Harris

The McGraw-Hill Companies

London · New York · St Louis · San Francisco · Auckland · Bogotá · Caracas
Lisbon · Madrid · Mexico · Milan · Montreal · New Delhi · Panama · Paris
San Juan · São Paulo · Singapore · Sydney · Tokyo · Toronto

Published by
McGRAW-HILL Publishing Company
Shoppenhangers Road, Maidenhead, Berkshire, SL6 2QL, England
Telephone: 01628 502500
Fax: 01628 770224

British Library Cataloguing in Publication Data
Harris, Jean
    Sharpen your team's skills in project management
    1. Industrial project management   2. Work groups
    I. Title
    658.4′04

    ISBN 0-07-709140-X

Library of Congress Cataloging-in-Publication Data
Harris, Jean
    Sharpen your team's skills in project management / Jean Harris.
        p.   cm. − (Sharpen your team's skills)
    Includes index.
    ISBN 0-07-709140-X (pbk. : alk. paper)
    1. Work groups−Training of.   2. Industrial project management.
    I. Title.   II. Series.
    HD66.H3745   1997
    658.3′124−dc20

                                                    96-41876
                                                    CIP

McGraw-Hill
A Division of The *McGraw·Hill* Companies

12345 CUP 9987

Typeset by BookEns Ltd, Royston, Herts
Printed and bound in Great Britain at the University Press, Cambridge

Printed on permanent paper in compliance with ISO Standard 9706

CONTENTS

Series Preface

This series of books focuses on sharpening the performance of your team by providing a range of training and support materials. These materials can be used in a variety of ways to improve the knowledge and skills of your team.

Creating high performance is achieved by paying attention to three key elements:

- The skills (competencies) of your people
- The way these skills are applied
- The support your people receive from you in applying their skills.

SKILL DEVELOPMENT

The books in this series will provide materials for the development of a range of skills on a subject-by-subject basis. Each book will provide information and exercises in manageable chunks (lessons), which will be presented in a format that will allow you to choose the most appropriate way to deliver them to your staff. The contents will consist of all you need to guide your staff to a full understanding of the subject.

There are at least four ways you could choose to guide the learning of your team:

- Training sessions
- Learning groups
- Open learning
- Experiential learning.

TRAINING SESSIONS

These can be run by bringing your people together and guiding them step by step through the materials, including the exercises. During these sessions you can invite your people to interact with you and the materials by asking questions and relating the materials to their current work. The materials will provide you with the detailed information you need to present the subject to your team.

LEARNING GROUPS

This approach involves dividing your team into small groups of two, three or four people and having a brief session with each group, in which you introduce them to the materials. Each group then works through the materials and meets with you from time to time to assess progress and receive your guidance.

OPEN LEARNING

This approach invites your people to use the materials at their own speed and in their own way. This is a form of individual learning which can be managed by regular meetings between you and your team as individuals or in a group. The process is started by introducing the materials to your team and agreeing some 'learning outcomes' to be achieved.

EXPERIENTIAL LEARNING

This calls for you to invite your team to examine the materials using the exercises as a focus, and then to get them to relate what they are learning directly to real-life situations in the workplace. This experience of the learning is then shared and discussed by the team as a whole.

The books in the series have been designed to enable these four approaches to be used, as well as other ways that you might think are more appropriate to your team's specific needs.

APPLYING SKILLS

Time spent developing skills can be wasted if people do not have the opportunity to practise them. It is important that you consider this aspect of performance before embarking on a particular programme. It is useful if you are able clearly to identify opportunities for practising skills and discuss these with your team. Providing opportunities for practising and further developing competency is part and parcel of the whole approach of this series.

PROVIDING SUPPORT

Once people have acquired a new skill and have been provided with opportunities to apply it, they still need your support and coaching while they are experimenting with using the skill. The opening book in this series, *Sharpen your skills in motivating people to perform*, provides clear guidance on how to help people to develop their skills and then how to provide experience, practice and support as they use these skills.

Before starting work with your team on the materials in this book I suggest you do the following:

1. Review the materials yourself.
2. Plan the approach you are going to follow.
3. Discuss with your team what you are planning.
4. Agree some learning outcomes.
5. Indicate how you are going to support your team during the learning process.

You can also make the materials relate to your specific circumstances by doing three things:

- Add local 'colour'
- Adjust the emphasis
- Integrate your own materials.

The authors in the series have endeavoured to provide a range of materials that is comprehensive and will support you and your team. I hope that during this process you learn from and enjoy the experience.

Dr Trevor J. Bentley
Series Editor

ABOUT THE EDITORIAL PANEL

Dr Trevor Bentley, series editor for this series, is a freelance organizational consultant, a facilitator and a writer. Prior to becoming a consultant and while working as a senior executive, Trevor carried out a major research project into decision making and organization structures for which he was awarded his PhD. Over the last 20 years he has had a wide range of experience working with organizations in over 20 countries. Trevor has trained for four years with Gestalt South West and attended Gestalt workshops in the UK and Europe. He now applies a Gestalt approach in his work.

Trevor has written 20 books and over 250 articles on business-related issues. His background includes careers as a management accountant, financial director, computer systems designer, management services manager, human computer interface consultant, trainer and business manager. His current area of interest is in the application of a Gestalt approach to solving problems of organizational harmony. This includes culture change, performance management, team facilitation, executive coaching, mentoring and integrated supervision.

Susan Clayton is a leading contributor to the use and development of Gestalt philosophy and practice in organizations. Focusing on human processes, she enables managers and their staff to achieve business goals that depend on managing people. Her skill in raising awareness of how people relate to each other can forge supportive alliances and powerful cooperative relationships. Her approach includes helping people to manage blocks and difficulties in their contact with others, clearing the way for work and business relationships to move forward and grow.

Susan works with managers at all levels. Her interventions have aided groups in turmoil, managers needing to reach common agreement and individuals needing mentoring and coaching support. She helps organizations understand how to manage in a way that creates trust, respect and clarity in human relationships.

Mike Taylor is a consultant involved in the design, implementation and facilitation of personal and team development programmes within organizations. After graduating in 1987, he worked with two outdoor management training providers, both as a manager and tutor. His work has a strong focus on the use of experiential learning in developing managers, mainly within larger organizations.

Mike also works with groups and single individuals in running meetings and events which help teams and individuals explore working practices and approaches. More recently he has developed an interest in Getalt as a way of understanding group processes. He is a member of the Association for Management Education and Development.

Dr Tony Voss is a counsellor, consultant and trainer. He originally trained as a chemist before working in environmental research developing sea-going computer systems and information technology, and later in the computer industry as a project manager, consultant and quality manager. Tony has a particular interest in enabling people to contribute fully and creatively to their endeavours, and sees this as benefiting individuals, their organizations and society at large. He is an Accredited Counsellor with the British Association for Counselling, and he also trained in Gestalt over a four-year period.

Tony works with those wanting to develop their organization and people, and those dealing with particular challenges in their working life. His clients also include those exploring the role of work in their life, as well as those with more personal issues.

ABOUT THE AUTHOR

After a ten-year career in the education sector Jean Harris made a number of career changes. She ran two national projects in the Schools Industry field for the City of Birmingham, worked in management services in the gas industry and was the Courseware Design Manager for Lucas Open Learning. In this role Jean and her team produced hundreds of hours of courseware to be delivered right across the Lucas organization to a wide range of personnel.

Since 1989, Jean has been a partner in Garner Harris Associates, a training, information and communications company. One of their main successes has been in the production of custom built courses for clients as diverse as British Aerospace, the Civil Aviation Authority, the DTI, Ford Motor Company, Royal Ordnance, Rover Group and Shell. This has involved dealing with a varied target audience in other European countries as well as the UK.

All of these course design activities will be costed and budgeted by Jean with the aim of delivering a quality product on time and within budget. Each project will also involve selecting suitable suppliers, and then managing the suppliers and budgets until completion.

Jean is a Fellow of the Association for Project Management, a Fellow of the Institute of Personnel and Development, is also involved in local and national committees and is currently President of the Solihull Chamber of Commerce and Industry.

CHAPTER 1

USING THIS BOOK AND HELPING PEOPLE TO LEARN

KEY LEARNING POINTS

- Understand the purpose of this book
- Know how it is structured
- Consider the ways in which you can make the best use of it

PURPOSE OF THIS BOOK

The purpose of this book is two-fold:

- To give you, the reader, a working knowledge of the basic techniques of project management
- To help you to share that knowledge with your team so that they can learn how to use these techniques.

If you have little or no experience of formal project management it will be a good starting point. If you have some experience but it is rusty or has been rather *ad hoc* and unplanned, this book will help you to use that experience in a more structured way.

This book does, however, assume that you have knowledge of basic management skills; for example that you will know how to

1

manage meetings or put together a simple action plan. Many of the project manager's skills are the skills of any good manager and we will explore this further in Chapter 3. Similarly, some of the techniques you will learn will not be new to you. Project management brings these together in a structured way to help you run projects efficiently and effectively. It is that structure which is the key to really *managing* your projects.

This book is not intended to be a manual on advanced project management. It will explain to you the basic techniques and how to use them. It will show how these techniques can benefit you. It will enable you to plan and manage projects of low to medium complexity. Hopefully those readers who will need to go on to more advanced techniques will see this basic introduction as a starting point and will want to go on from here to learn more.

Many of the project manager's skills are the skills of any good manager

THE ROLE OF THE MANAGER

To gain the most benefit from the people in their team a good manager will help their people to perform well. If the manager is motivating and managing performance this will help the team to give their best. Self development with management support and guidance is one of the keys to improved performance. This may require helping the team to gain and use new skills – and sometimes these will be skills which the manager does not yet possess.

Managers and others embarked on self development can use this book to gain knowledge about the topic themselves, then use the exercises to share that learning in a practical way.

Managers can use this book to gain knowledge about the topic themselves, then use the exercises to share that learning in a practical way

USING THIS BOOK

Each chapter covers a different aspect of project management. The knowledge builds up sequentially, so even if you feel you know a particular topic well we would advise you to read through the relevant chapter to refresh your memory and fit it into the whole context of a project management structure.

EXERCISES

At the end of each chapter you will find a training session outlined with exercises or activities. Those at the end of Chapters 1 and 2 are to help you consolidate the learning in those chapters. The exercises at the end of all the remaining chapters are for you to work through with your team. We would advise you to read the chapter carefully then familiarize yourself with the exercises before you carry them out with the team. To help your planning you will find notes for each session describing:

- Exercise overview
- Equipment and materials required
- Suggested methods
- Likely time required.

You will need to introduce each session by explaining the topic to your team. There are four possible ways of doing this:

1. Make notes as you read through the chapter. Turn these into a script or cue cards and give a summary at the beginning of the learning session.
2. Make notes as you read through the chapter. Turn these into a list of key points and write this up as a handout for the team to read before each session.
3. Ask one team member to read the chapter in advance of the session and ask him or her to carry out points 1 or 2 above. You also need to make your own notes to ensure that they cover everything, or so you could cover if they are off sick on the day of your team session.

    Rotate this task so everyone takes part and the workload is spread.
4. Any combination of these three.

If you are not confident about explaining each topic to your team, you may decide to ask them to read parts of the book before each learning session.

    Most of the exercises are designed to last about 15–30 minutes, but you can control this by deciding how long you will allow for brainstorming or discussion. Each session should last 1–1½ hours in total. The methods we suggest are nothing more sophisticated than a flip chart and brainstorming technique. Most of the exercises are particularly suitable for groups of about 6 to 12 people. A few more or less will not matter, but groups larger than 15 make it difficult for everyone to contribute, so you may be better splitting the team up into smaller groups for parts of the session.

    Few of the exercises have a 'right' or 'wrong' answer, so you will not find solutions or model answers. In some cases the solutions are reflecting on past experiences and learning from these, in others they will be planning what you need to do to carry out your work or deciding what techniques will work best with your team.

CAPTURE THE INFORMATION

At the end of each learning session ask one or two team members to write up key outcomes from the exercises as a set of notes or bullet points for circulation to all team members. Again, rotate the task to share the workload.

WORKING THROUGH THE CHAPTERS AND SESSIONS

Exactly how you work through the book, whether you ask your team to read all or parts of it, whether you read the whole book before you begin any of the team exercises or not, is entirely up to you.

Some of the exercises in later chapters build on ones carried out earlier. It will be helpful, therefore, if you keep the charts and notes you and your team produce in each working session, label them with the chapter name and store them for easy access later.

Chapters 6, 7 and 10 are long and quite complex and you may prefer to read these more than once before you tackle the learning sessions with your team. The exercises are also quite long so you may prefer to break these into two sessions.

HELPING PEOPLE TO LEARN

You may not be a trainer, but as a manager you will probably have experience in coaching or mentoring. You will almost certainly have experience in managing people. As part of your management role you are in a position to help your team to learn. You can do this in a number of ways; to some extent this will depend on your own management style and the relationship you have with your team. If you have an ongoing programme of coaching and learning together, working through this book will be easier. If you are new to helping people to learn or wish to introduce a new approach, it may be worthwhile looking at this topic in more depth before you do any exercises with your team.

As part of your management role you are in a position to help your team to learn

Although each of the exercises in this book has notes on how to use it, some general guidelines on helping your team may also be helpful. We would recommend the following strategies to help you:

1. Plan and prepare yourself well for each session.
2. Make sure you give your team the impression that learning together is important to you – not something imposed on you against your will.
3. Value all contributions – encourage people to talk and share their experiences. This pool of experience is a valuable asset to all the team.
4. Give the learning the time it requires.

SESSION 1 – EXERCISES FOR YOURSELF

OVERVIEW
This session is intended to help you plan how you will use this book to work with your team. It only involves you.

EQUIPMENT AND MATERIALS
For each of these exercises you will only require this book, and a pen.

You may wish to start a folder for *project management training* and keep all the notes on these exercises and the team exercises together. If so, now would be the best time to start this.

TIME
All three exercises should together take about 20–30 minutes.

Exercise 1.1

Before you begin the next chapter spend a few minutes looking at the book contents on page v. Using the chapter titles and headings as a guide, assess your own knowledge of project management and make a list of the areas where you feel you need most help. The matrix-type table below gives an example of part of such a list.

Topic	Existing skill level	Help required	Outcome
1. Helping others to learn	Moderate	Talk to HR re: further reading list	Done 6.6.96
2. Project manage-ment – general	Moderate	None	
3. Role of project manager	Moderate –low	Read Chapter 3 carefully. Talk to Tom S re: his experience	
4.			

As you read through the book go back to this list and tick off the topics when you feel confident that you could explain the main components of the technique to someone else.

This could be the first section of your project management training folder. If you are not starting a folder, keep this list somewhere accessible (inside this book or in your Filofax™, for example).

Exercise 1.2

Steps

Bearing in mind your own knowledge and the time you think it will take you to work through each chapter, consider how you want to use the book; we have listed some possible options below. You will see that there are many ways in which you can tackle this book and some of the options can be used alongside others.

- Read through the entire book then work through team exercises, one chapter per week.
- Work through team exercises as they are reached at the end of each chapter from 3–14.
- Read through the entire book, give the team the task of reading one chapter at a time and then doing the exercises as they reach them. Discuss in group weekly or monthly meetings.
- Write summaries of each chapter to give to the team before undertaking the exercises.
- Plan a timetable for team meetings and organize necessary reading to fit in with this.

Add other options you may think of yourself. Decide which you want to use and note your planned method in your project management training folder.

Exercise 1.3

Steps

Working through this book and sharing your learning with your team could be seen as a project in itself. That being the case, it requires some, albeit minimal, planning at this stage:

1. List in your training folder three or four outcomes which you wish to see at the end of this project; include at least one for

yourself and one for your team. Number or label each one.
2. Draw up a simple action plan to help you to put into practice what you have learned. The pro forma below might help. The second column relates to the list of outcomes above.

Action	Outcome/ desires	Responsibility	Time required	Completion by
Read intro and Chapters 1–2		Self		
Read Chapter 3		Self		
Carry out exercises in Chapter 3		Self and team		

Put the action plan in your training folder or with your other notes from Exercises 1.1, 1.2 and 1.3.

SUMMARY

This book will give you a good working knowledge of basic project management. It will also provide you with the means to share that with your team, so developing their knowledge and skills.

Each of the chapters covers a different aspect of the topic, building up your knowledge as you work through it.

LEARNING SESSIONS

The learning sessions at the end of Chapters 1 and 2 are for your own use, but all the rest are for you to work through with your team. Each session describes exercises for you to use and gives guidance on how to use them.

Exactly how you use this book is up to you, but we suggest that you:

1. Start a training folder to keep a record of the learning which takes place.
2. At the end of each learning session ask one or two team members to summarize in the form of handouts.

3. Use the main body of each chapter as prior learning and reference for yourself and also for the team if you wish.

HELPING PEOPLE TO LEARN

You are in a position to help your team to learn most effectively. You can do this by:

- Being well prepared for each session
- Showing your team that you value learning and that it is important
- Making use of the contributions from all team members in a constructive way
- Allowing time for learning.

CHAPTER 2

WHAT'S IN IT FOR ME?

KEY LEARNING POINTS

- Understand why projects can fail
- Know the three key benefits of correctly managing a project
- Know a simple definition of a project
- Know a simple definition of project management

PROJECT FAILURES

If you were planning a major project at home, such as installing a new fitted kitchen, you would have certain expectations. You would probably expect to have a kitchen which matched the specification you agreed (colour, materials, structure and so on), at the cost you agreed and delivered and installed when you agreed.

If the supplier did not deliver on time but everything else was as expected when it was finally fitted, would the project be a failure?
If it cost more than you had planned, would the project be a failure?
If the kitchen was the wrong colour, would the project be a failure?
If it all fell apart in six months' time, would the project be a failure?

You would probably say 'yes' to the last question but may have said 'no' or be unsure about the other three. The situation is that in *all* these cases the project could be said to have failed. A truly successful project should be delivered on time, to cost and to the exact specification agreed.

There have been many spectacular instances of projects which have failed – the Sydney Opera House, Concorde, the Advance Passenger Train and the Channel Tunnel. These projects did eventually get completed but they failed in one or more aspects of their plans – they were late, overran the original budgets or were not delivered to the planned specification.

Getting all three aspects right is not easy – sometimes it may seem impossible – but there are ways to avoid potential failures. One way is by learning from the mistakes of the past – others' as well as your own.

A truly successful project should be delivered on time, to cost and to the exact specification agreed

Getting all three aspects right is not easy. One way is by learning from the mistakes of the past – other's as well as your own

WHY DID THEY FAIL?

The reasons for failure may not always be easy to find, but we will look here at one example to examine some possible causes.

CONCORDE

The major failure of the Concorde project was the cost overrun. The original estimate was £95 million in 1959. The final development cost was £1140 million, plus production costs of about £700 million to the end of 1978. In fact the final costs were over four times the total 'official' estimates! Even as the project was progressing the estimates of costs were rising.

The time plan for the project did not fare much better. The original estimate was six years, but Concorde eventually took some fifteen years to come to fruition. Why, then, was this allowed to happen? There is not one simple reason; the answer is a complex combination of many factors. It may be unlikely that you are planning to design and build a revolutionary form of transport – but some of the lessons from the Concorde project are just as applicable to smaller or less ambitious projects.

First, this was a project with a large element of research and development, so it was inevitable that there were many unknown factors. The end result, even, is not known. Research budgets are usually established on an annual basis, or some other arbitrary time basis, whereby it is agreed that a certain amount of work (personnel, materials and so on) will be funded over this period. The money available to spend may or may not produce results. Then as the project moves into the 'development' stage the end results may still be uncertain. In these types of project there is a 'learning' element throughout the research and development stages. This is the case in most projects in the aircraft industry and it was certainly true of Concorde. If you don't know what your end product is going to be, how can you cost it accurately? The answer is you can't – but you can take steps to make your predictions more accurate.

The most useful principle is to examine past experiences carefully. Collect *all* the available data from past projects and *use* it. If all past projects have overrun by 400 per cent, is it then sensible to say 'but we'll do better' and only multiply your original estimate by two? Learn to accept the experience of others and analyse their experience sensibly and realistically. Take into account *all* of the salient facts, such as inflation and what will happen to this if time overruns?

Other projects can also have an effect on the main project, for example the cancellation of the TSR-2 project had an enormous effect on the Concorde project. The Olympus engine intended for Concorde, was also intended to power the TSR-2. So when TSR-2 was cancelled, all the subsequent costs were borne entirely by the Concorde project.

When the Concorde budget was set the past experience of the Treasury was not even examined

When the Concorde budget was set the past experience of the Treasury was not even examined. Those who had the small amount of useful knowledge available were just not consulted.

The first forecasts for time schedules on Concorde were far too optimistic. The commercial availability of Concorde was delayed by nearly five years, mainly due to design and technical problems. This meant lost sales and less income – so affecting cost. Again, lessons could have been learned from the past and some of the reasons for delay foreseen.

The key qualitative effects of the project (time and cost) were negative, and the problems with one exacerbated the other. However, it cannot be denied that the end result is a technical triumph, still flying after more than 20 years. The USA, by contrast, abandoned their SST (Supersonic Transport) project in 1971 after spending $500 million. The Concorde project spent £1490 million (net outlay) and the UK and France have 14 operational aircraft. So who is better off? If cost was the most important factor, the USA; but if the end project is more important, then the UK and France have benefited.

It could be said that on qualitative grounds the Concorde project *was* a success; or, perhaps, a technical success but a commercial failure? It all depends on what the project's objectives were.

LEARNING FROM THE PAST

So many of us are obsessed with the need to succeed that we try to forget our failures. Projects which fail are filed away and forgotten. But that is denying the one potential success of projects that fail – they can help future success by teaching us valuable lessons.

Every experience I have had I treat as a learning experience. All project managers should do the same. Whenever something has gone wrong there is a reason for it. If you can establish that reason, next time you should be able to take steps to avoid a repeat of the same problem. Use the experience of others as well as your own and use that experience to learn.

One potential success of projects that fail is that they can help future success by teaching us valuable lessons

WHAT IS A PROJECT?

Projects can cover many activities from small short-term ones to multi-billion pound projects lasting many years. Writing a book, refitting a kitchen, making a dinner, building a motorway – all could be described as projects.

The common elements are that they:

- have definite start and finish points
- involve a variety of tasks, activities or events
- involve a number of different resources.

Anything with a definite beginning and end, involving a number of activities could be described as a project. So moving to a new office would be a project, but the ongoing activities of running the office day to day would not.

Some projects are new or 'one-offs', some are repeats of similar exercises carried out in the past. Apart from the broad definition given above there will be certain common features in projects of a similar nature. For example, a project to produce a new product will involve design, testing, setting up a production facility and so on. But the detail will vary according to resources, timescale and individuals involved. So each new project needs to be planned and controlled in its own way, but the *principles* of how you do this will be the same and this book aims to show you these. The detail will vary – and that is where your own experience and the experience of your team will help you develop and improve your skills.

Anything with a definite beginning and end, involving a number of activities could be described as a project

WHY MANAGE A PROJECT?

Any task which is well managed is likely to run smoothly and produce good results. Managing your own time and your own money are small examples. If you manage your projects well there are benefits to be gained beyond the amount of effort you have to put in. One of the biggest benefits I have seen personally in managing a project is the reduction of the 'hassle' factor. The following example could apply to any industry:

I was asked to organize the distribution of 200 packages to about 200 individuals or departments on six different sites of one company. All packages included three common elements plus one other (a video) which varied according to the department. The deliveries had to go out on different dates. By staggering the arrival of the videos at the warehouse we ensured that the right video went in the right pack. By also printing out the labels for the packs on a staggered basis we helped to avoid the wrong packs going on the wrong vans. All this required planning but saved a lot of angry customers getting the wrong packs.

The one element I forgot was to warn the sites when the goods were to arrive. The first drop was to a small site with only one main gate, so this went well. The next was a different matter – a large site with several gates and more than one 'goods inwards' facility. The result was the van driver spending $2\frac{1}{2}$ hours getting sent from place to place and no one agreeing to accept the load!

The van driver got hassle from various security guards, the customer was angry because his packages were late and I got hassle from the van driver and the customer!

A bit more planning could have pre-empted the problem and avoided the hassle. The benefits of better planning would have been to me (the individual), the van driver (the team), the customer (the organization).

Planning is only part of the process – controlling the project by constant monitoring is also essential. How would you know if your project is successful without a control mechanism? Looking at an example in banking you might ask why did some BCCI directors manage for so long to get away with taking money out of the bank for unauthorized use? Because there was no system to *control* what was happening.

Another example to illustrate this can be seen in a process industry – oil refining. In an oil refinery there are thousands of pipes, towers and vessels carrying liquids and gases at varying

Planning is only part of the process – controlling the project by constant monitoring is also essential

pressures and temperatures. The pressure, volume, temperature and other parameters of all these vessels are monitored regularly and the result logged. But what happens to these results? They must be used to *control* the process. You could log the fact that pressure is building up in a vessel until it explodes – but that is not very helpful! You must have a mechanism for using the data you are getting and this is where the control element comes in.

These examples are from ongoing activities, but they are no less valuable in teaching us lessons for project management. In two very different industries we can see that control is an essential element of success.

MANAGING FOR SUCCESS

The examples we have looked at earlier show why and how things can go wrong. But is there a key factor in stopping things going wrong? Yes – that factor is in managing your project.

We could use a simple analogy as an example. If you are going on a journey but you are not quite sure what time you want to arrive, exactly where you are going or what method of transport you will use, the chances of you ending up in the right place at the right time are pretty slim! If you know where you want to be and when, then plan your transport to fit in with your budget, you are more likely to succeed. If you constantly check your progress en route (Is this the correct train? Is it on time? Are we on the right road? and so on) and adjust as necessary, you are almost certain of success. This is the *management* of the journey – planning, monitoring and control. So project management could be defined as:

> **the oversight and organization necessary to ensure that the project is completed on schedule, within budget and to specification.**

We will expand on this later in the book. You may then prefer to write your own definition, in your own words.

WHAT ARE THE BENEFITS?

It is obvious from the description of project failures that the potential for disaster is great. But what if it goes well – what are the benefits? This may seem obvious but it is worth spelling out at this point – if all those involved are not aware of the potential benefits they may be less able or willing to contribute the not inconsiderable effort required for success.

THE ORGANIZATION

To the organization that required the project the benefits of success are:

- it gets what it wanted (*to specification*)
- it gets it when it is needed (*on time*)
- it gets it at the agreed budget (*to cost*).

This can give it commercial success and enhance its position in the marketplace. This will enable the organization to work more efficiently in future by using the project management techniques to improve its systems. It will enable it to plan its work and activities using the project's outcomes; it can accurately plan cash flow and budgets and so spend sensibly for future development.

THE TEAM

When things are going well, a team is functioning well. A well-planned and managed project will enable the team to make the best use of their skills. It will:

- increase effectiveness
- decrease frustration and stress
- bring harmony
- enhance job satisfaction.

THE INDIVIDUAL

The personal satisfaction and esteem which comes from success may be obvious, as will be the lack of stress. If organizations are successful all within will benefit from more work and better security, so individuals also benefit indirectly from an organization's success. If your project is a success then *you* are going to benefit; you personally, as well as your team and your organization. Business is more competitive than ever – no one can afford to fail and finding ways to avoid failure has got to be worthwhile. If these ways also make life easier then the benefits are even more worthwhile. So a successful project benefits the individual by bringing:

- greater self esteem
- greater job security
- lack of stress and frustration.

SESSION 2 – EXERCISES FOR YOURSELF

OVERVIEW

Before you can share the benefits of project management with your team you need to understand these for yourself. These first exercises are for you to do on your own and they will help you with this understanding.

EQUIPMENT AND MATERIALS

You will need this book, paper, pen and your project management training folder (if you plan to use one). You will also need the results of Exercise 1.3.

TIME

All four exercises should take about 30–40 minutes in total.

Exercise 2.1

Consider any project with which you have been involved or which you know well. This can be work related or home based, anything from moving office to building a wall, installing a new IT system to moving house. Write down the name of your project then answer the following questions.

1. How many people were involved?
2. Were the desired outcomes of the project clear from the outset?
3. Were the outcomes achieved (wholly or partially)?
4. Would you consider the project a success or failure?
5. On what grounds did it succeed or fail?
6. Was any planning undertaken at the outset?
7. By whom and with whom was it shared?
8. How, if at all, was the project monitored?
9. Was this monitoring qualitative or quantitative?
10. Was it used to control the project in any way?

Exercise 2.2

Steps

Now look back at your answers to the questions above. Working on the basis of learning by past experiences, let us think more about that project:

1. First think about questions 1 and 2 and consider what improvements you could have made. For example, would clearer outcomes have been helpful? In what ways?
2. Thinking about your answers to questions 3–5, if the project was a complete success was this by accident or the result of good management?
   — If it was due to good management can you identify and list the factors which contributed?
   — If it was by accident can you identify and list any factors which would have made it easier or *more* successful?
3. Now think about your answers to the rest of the questions:
   — If it was *not* a success can you identify and list the reasons why it failed (not just the end result such as cost overrun, but the underlying causes).
   — Would better management have helped and in what ways?

Exercise 2.3

Look back at the action plan you prepared for Exercise 1.3. In the light of the answers you have given in Exercise 2.2, do you want to add to or alter this plan in any way now? If so, do that before you read on.

Exercise 2.4

As part of your preparation for discussion with your team, write some notes under the heading 'An introduction to project management'. You can use the information in Chapters 1 and 2 to help you.

SUMMARY

PROJECT FAILURES

The measurement of a project's success will depend on its objectives. Projects can be considered as failures for a variety of reasons, but if a project fails to achieve any of its objectives it can be said to be a failure.

In the past research and development projects have been notoriously difficult to plan accurately and they have a poor track record of success. While it may be extremely difficult to plan a project where the final outcome is uncertain the errors can be minimized. The best way to do this is to:

- talk to those with past experience
- collect all the available data
- not be complacent and assume you can always do better
- consider the track record of previous projects
- learn the lessons from the past.

PROJECT DEFINITION

A project is a series of activities or tasks which has a beginning, a middle and an end and which involves a number of different resources.

MANAGING THE PROJECT

To ensure success a project must be planned, monitored and controlled. Without this management element it is unlikely, if not impossible, to fully achieve all the project objectives successfully.

BENEFITS

A well-managed and successful project will bring benefits to the individual, the team and the organization.

CHAPTER 3

WHAT IS A PROJECT MANAGER?

KEY LEARNING POINTS

- Know the meaning of project management
- Understand the purpose of managing projects
- Understand the role of the project manager
- Know some of the attributes of a good project manager

WHAT IS PROJECT MANAGEMENT?

The concept of project management as a tool was probably first devised in the nineteenth century, although it is practically impossible to pinpoint exactly when this method of organization evolved. Looking back at our definition of a project, there are many historical activities which can be described as projects – the building of Hadrian's Wall by the Romans and even earlier building projects like the Great Wall of China and the Pyramids would easily fit the criteria for *projects*. However, we do know that some form of project management was used by the Victorian engineers and the industrialization of Britain was certainly helped by project management.

It is only since the 1950s that project management has been recognized as a 'science' or management tool in its own right. The roots of modern project management can be found in the Polaris Missile project of 1956. Since then the tool has been refined and developed and is now a skill which we can apply to projects of any budget or size.

Project management is the skill of using these tools and techniques to organize activities to achieve a specific purpose. It should include many good general management skills – communication, interpersonal skills, budgeting and so on – but over and above these are the specific planning and controlling techniques we will address in this book.

The roots of modern project management can be found in the Polaris Missile project of 1956. Since then the tool has been refined and developed

PROJECT MANAGERS

PAST TIMES

Looking back on the industrial history of any developed country we are often awed by the achievements of people in the past. They moved events forward in tremendous leaps without the modern equipment we have access to now. For example, much has been discussed and written about how the great stones were transported to Stonehenge and pulled into their upright position without the aid of heavy duty lorries or cranes. We have probably all seen drawings of thousands of slaves toiling over the construction of the great Egyptian Pyramids. But have you ever thought about how this was managed and organized?

Unfortunately, we do not have access to the project plans for the Pyramids or the standing stones at Stonehenge, but we do have some information on more recent constructions in Britain. The civil engineers of Victorian times did not have access to the sophisticated scientific techniques of project management available today. Nor did they have the modern communication and computing equipment to help them. Even without these, some of the Victorian engineers managed their projects successfully and were extremely efficient. This shows that the underlying skills are more significant in the success of projects than the modern technology. The sophistication we have today is an enhancement and should save us some of the drudgery ('number crunching' in particular). But in the end it is the people who do the work.

Brunel was a hopeless delegator; he could not motivate other people and he did not know how to handle sub-contractors. Although he did eventually complete most of his projects, he was a

Unfortunately, we do not have access to the project plans for the Pyramids or the standing stones at Stonehenge

poor project manager. By contrast, Joseph Locke was a first-class project manager. He controlled huge numbers of men and horses without the aid of computers, yet still completed the Lancaster to Carlisle Railway on time and within budget.

These examples show that the human role in project management must be at least as important as the technology. Now we have established the technology, we must not forget the human factor. The role of the project manager in managing and motivating the project team cannot be overstressed.

So, what does a project manager do? Let us consider some examples.

The human role on project management must be at least as important as the technology

EVERYDAY LIFE

In Chapter 2 we mentioned refitting a kitchen as an example of a project. If we consider this in more depth, we can identify the role of the project manager. The scenario could go like this:

> The householder has decided that the kitchen is scruffy and inefficient and needs replacing. She looks around at different kitchens available to get an idea of cost and decides she can afford a new kitchen – but not a handmade expensive one.
>
> She sets her budget, arranges where the money is coming from, decides upon the suppliers of various components and the local builder to install it.
>
> She orders the various components and commissions the builder. She agrees time and cost with suppliers, then checks parts when they arrive, oversees the work to ensure it is to the standard she wants. When invoices come in she checks these against the quote and pays them if they are satisfactory.

In short, the householder is managing this project – planning, budgeting, monitoring and controlling, then finally signing it off. If she has planned well, got good suppliers, explained clearly what she wants, budgeted accurately and so on, the project should be a success.

BUSINESS PROJECTS

When managing projects at work, the same basic principles apply, but these are usually more complex and the project manager may not have such a free hand to make decisions early on. For example, the budget may be set by someone else; the completion date may be decided by others before she is given the project; the suppliers or sub-contractors may not be of her choosing. She still has to undertake the same tasks to get the project completed successfully – but she may have to bring into play a wider variety of management skills to do it.

WHAT IS A GOOD PROJECT MANAGER?

The simple answer to this is:

One who delivers on time, within budget and to the agreed specification.

The difference lies in how this is achieved. Some project managers manage to do this and still keep everyone happy, some achieve it at the cost of upsetting and alienating many others. As the old saying goes, 'it is not possible to please all the people all of the time' – nor should we always want to. A good project manager has the skills to achieve the aims of the project while leaving those involved with a sense of their achievement and contribution as well.

In the exercises at the end of this chapter we will explore the qualities of a good project manager further.

WHAT DOES THE MANAGER MANAGE?

It would seem patently obvious that the project manager manages the project – but what is *the project*? The project comprises *all* of its component parts and the most valuable (also often the most problematical) are its resources. Much of this is in the form of people. We saw earlier in the case of Brunel and Locke that the best people manager was also the best project manager. This is no less true today.

No matter what sophisticated tools you use for planning and monitoring, it is the people who make the project happen. Without their expertise and goodwill, it will not work. Let us look at an example:

> The project had already been started but the client realized it was running into problems. He had commissioned a number of suppliers but had never brought them together as a team. They were all experienced in their fields and good at what they did and he had assumed that they would continue to perform as they had for one-off tasks previously.

When he realized that the project was running into problems, the client appointed an experienced project manager to take over the project.

One key supplier had assumed that he was the lead supplier and therefore driving the project. It was true that his role was a key one and very few other tasks could proceed without his prior input. When the new project manager, James, was brought on board, he first went to see this key supplier with the client. It was made clear by the client that James was now managing the project and had the authority to do this. Over the next couple of weeks, meetings were arranged with other suppliers and (for the first time) real objectives set for the project, even though this process slowed things down initially.

It was obvious from the outset that the key supplier resented James' presence and although lip service was paid to his role, they seemed determined to carry on as before in their *ad hoc* way, delivering what they wanted (not exactly what the client had asked for) and when they were ready.

After several of these failures, the project manager's patience was getting very short. A long discussion with the head of the supplier company had resulted in a short-term improvement, but this soon lapsed. James would have preferred to pay off the supplier and replace them with one he knew could perform as required, but this was not an option – and the supplier knew this! There were other possible options open:

1. Let the project fail, then blame the supplier
2. Bring in a back-up supplier and do the work twice at double the cost
3. Sort out the problem supplier
4. Put in some other back-up system.

Option 1 was not desirable; James had been brought in to manage the project and believed that any failure would be his failure. Blaming somebody else was not acceptable. Late delivery would affect a new process and thousands of employees.

Option 2 was not possible; James did not have complete control of the budget and some suppliers were being paid directly by the client. He was not, therefore, able to move funds around to pay an additional supplier.

Option 3 had already failed but he kept plugging away at it to try to get better results. This meant winning the confidence of the supplier to let him see that success was in *his* best interests.

Option 4 was possible and James revisited the objectives,

revised the outcomes, discussed these with the client and thereby moved the problem supplier off the critical path wherever possible by offering alternative deliverables.

The project outcomes were:

1. All the agreed objectives were met and additional outcomes achieved
2. The project was delivered on time
3. The project ran about 20 per cent over budget.

So what can be learn from this? There are a number of factors which contributed to the problem.

1. At the outset, the suppliers were not brought together to discuss the project and form a team.
2. The project manager had no input in selecting the team.
3. No clear objectives had been set and agreed at the outset.
4. The change implicit in another supplier being brought in to manage the project caused resentment in one key person.
5. The project manager did not have enough authority to make all the decisions he needed to.

Whether or not what the project manager did was the best solution is a question for discussion, but some important lessons can be learned. The good techniques this project manager used can be summarized as follows. When you have project problems:

1. Look back at the original objectives and consider alternative routes to achieve the same ends.
2. Look at the three criteria – quality, cost and time (which we will look at in more detail in Chapter 5) – and prioritize these. Are any flexible?
3. Look at the people and find better ways to get what you want out of them.

You may be able to think of other solutions, but, in particular, this case highlights the importance of the role of people – the manager and everyone involved working as a team. We will come back to this in Chapter 4. It also highlights the importance of the way the project manager is allowed to manage – if anyone is to have the accountability, then they must also be given the authority to make the necessary decisions.

SESSION 3 – EXERCISES WITH YOUR TEAM

OVERVIEW

The following exercises are intended to be worked through with your team.

You can use the list of management skills drawn up in Exercise 3.2 to help you to use Exercise 3.3 to identify any training needs which potential project managers may have.

EQUIPMENT AND MATERIALS

You will require a room for your team meeting and a flip chart, with pens. (For all of these exercises, an overhead projector and foils can be used instead of a flip chart.) For each exercise you need to appoint a 'scribe' to make notes on the flip chart. Seating should be arranged so all the team can see the flip chart and each other. An open 'U' formation or semi-circle are probably the best ways to achieve this.

PREPARATION

Read through the exercises before the team session.

For Exercise 3.2 start two new flip charts. Head them 'Helpful or constructive' and 'Unhelpful or destructive'.

METHOD

The following exercises are all carried out by discussion and brainstorming. If your team is not familiar with this technique, you may wish to begin by describing the rules of brainstorming:

1. *All* contributions are accepted and written up.
2. They are paraphrased or abbreviated only with the consent of the contributor.
3. Contributions are not criticized or commented on at the outset.
4. There is no discussion during the brainstorm.
5. A time limit is set and only exceeded if the group is still contributing new ideas.
6. Discussion and comment follow when the 'brainstorm' is complete.

TIME

Exercise 3.1 should take approximately 30–40 minutes, Exercise 3.2 should take approximately 30–40 minutes and Exercise 3.3 should take approximately 15–20 minutes.

Exercise 3.1

Steps

1. Consider two projects at work; one successful, one a failure or with a lot of problems. Discuss the choice with the team, when chosen, and write the title of each on a separate flip chart.
2. On each flip chart, list the following headings:
   — Aims
   — What was achieved?
   — Why was it:
     — Successful?
     — Unsuccessful?

   Now brainstorm to add the information to these headings for each topic (5–10 minutes).
3. Next, from points listed under point 3, try to identify those points which are related to the management of the project. Do this by team discussion (15–20 minutes).

Exercise 3.2

Steps

You will need the flip chart you have prepared with the headings 'Helpful or constructive' and 'Unhelpful or destructive'. By group discussion (10–15 minutes) take each point in turn from the previous Exercise, 3.1, then ask the team to:

1. Divide the list drawn up about management of the project in Exercise 3.1 into two new lists, then:
   — Identify and list all the helpful and constructive things that happened.
   — Identify and list all the destructive or unhelpful things that happened.
2. Again by team discussion for 5–10 minutes, consider the role of the project manager in these successes or failures.

From the lists drawn up in point 1, draw up a new list headed 'attributes of a good project manager', and for each of the attributes brainstorm to draw up a list of any management skills that you believe contribute to this. This should take a further 10–15 minutes. An example is given below.

Attributes of a good project manager	Management skills
Good communication	Listening Clear simple memos Regular personal contact

Exercise 3.3

Steps

This exercise can be carried out individually or one-to-one. The team/group part of this session should take 15–20 minutes and should allow time for the team to question you or each other. If you prefer you could discuss this on a one-to-one basis, or you could ask individuals to identify their own training needs.

Ask each team member to list all the attributes in their training file. Next to each one they should note their opinion of their own skills and training needs. You can then either:

1. Ask them to discuss this with a colleague of their choice and refine it, then give you a list of what training they believe they need.
2. Ask them to each share their lists with you on a one-to-one basis.

For your own future reference you could produce a skills matrix, as shown below:

Name	Skill 1	Skill 2	Skill 3
Joe Bloggs	A/1	A/2	C/1
Ann Brown	B/1	A/2	C/3

Key
A = Achieved to good standard already
B = Needs some additional experience or training
C = No experience
1 = Skill essential
2 = Some experience useful
3 = Skill not required

We will come back to this again in Chapter 4.

SUMMARY

PROJECT MANAGEMENT

This is the skill of utilizing the resources, money and time available to deliver a project on time, within budget and to specification.

THE PROJECT MANAGER

The project manager exercises his or her skills to manage the project. Although technology can be used as a tool in this management, past experience has shown that people management is the most essential single element in delivering a successful project.

THE ROLE OF THE PROJECT MANAGER

The project manager should have senior enough status to be given the authority as well as the accountability to manage the project. Senior management should support the project manager to maintain this authority as well as the motivation required. A good project manager will consider all the requirements of the project at the planning stage, monitor these throughout and be flexible when unexpected things happen.

CHAPTER 4

*T*HE PROJECT

TEAM

KEY LEARNING POINTS

- Understand the importance of human factors in good project management
- Know the qualities of a good project manager
- Know how to select a project team
- Understand the importance of allocating tasks
- Understand the value of empowering team members
- Know why good communication is essential for success

THE HUMAN SIDE OF PROJECTS

So far we have looked briefly at the role of the project manager and systems for planning and control of projects. Effective project systems are only part of the story, good human relations systems are the other part. If you have good human relations on a project you can expect reasonable performance. If this breaks down you can never achieve good project performance, no matter how good the technical systems are.

Good human relations systems are equally as important as effective project systems

If there are technical problems on a project there are usually ways of solving them, but people problems are much more difficult to solve. We stated in Chapter 3 that the earliest project managers who were also good people managers were the most successful.

Today, even with all the sophisticated computer programs and other tools available to us, this is still true.

The normal patterns of behaviour in management are accentuated in the management of projects. So, if a project manager is aware of basic human management skills and willing to learn he or she can learn more and learn more quickly through managing projects than through normal management processes.

The human problems in projects arise because of the complex and sometime ambiguous nature of the matrix organization in projects. This can be made even more difficult if the authority of the project manager is not clear. His or her lines of authority or influence are often fitted alongside a traditional pyramidal organizational structure, cutting across the usual vertical lines of command and boundaries around departments. In an earlier example we touched on the value of dedicated teams with members located together. Another example is the case of the Land Rover Discovery project:

This vehicle was brought to the market in 35 months – then (1989) a European record for a new model.

Although the personnel involved in the project still had lines to their functional departments, it was made clear that the project team was a priority and the project manager had the authority to carry out the task in hand.

The production of Discovery grew from 10 000 in 1989 to 30 000 in 1992. By 1993 it was the company's main product and contributed to a billion pound revenue generator. This growth in production has been facilitated by the company's TQI policy and some very interesting developments in team working.

Cultural changes

Total quality   The whole philosophy of Rover Group is one of quality throughout the organization. Many techniques are used to encourage this.

Empowerment   The 'fact holders' (that is, those who have the knowledge) also have the power to put in place changes and developments which they see as necessary to improve their work. The management team has not abdicated responsibility but has empowered the teams.

Ownership   The only two things which matter are the people and the products. At all levels those involved own the consequences of their actions.

Business orientation Better communications ensure that everyone knows more about the whole business so that anyone who makes a decision understands the full implications of that decision.

Communication Information about the business is passed out to all personnel. The main methods for these are the Rover Group company newsletter, monthly Land Rover company brief and team boards for local information, which are updated daily.

Common objectives Across the whole site (powertrain; body and assembly) everyone is working towards commonly accepted objectives.

A learning environment Training and sharing of experience is an essential part of the culture in the company.

THE PROJECT MANAGER

The project manager should have overall responsibility for planning, monitoring and controlling the various elements

The project manager should have the overall responsibility for the project. They should have the expertise to plan the project, monitor it overall and control the various elements.

The project manager does not work within the normal superior–subordinate relationships. They have to manage their peers, juniors and superiors in other departments and companies contributing to the project. Personnel in these departments or companies must work for two managers, the project manager and their own department or company manager. This will require the project manager to gain the commitment and loyalty of the team. The one thing that binds them together are the project objectives. It is the skill of the good project manager which engenders that commitment and loyalty.

In addition to these human relations skills the project manager must have the ability to carry out the tasks specific to the project. They may need help in specific areas, such as finance, particularly with very long or complex projects. But they should still have an overview of what is happening in enough detail to maintain overall control.

Also, very importantly, they must have the authority to *manage*. If they are to be accountable for the project they must be empowered to make key decisions on costs, manpower, sub-contractors and other suppliers.

We have already considered some of the attributes of a good project manager in Chapter 3. To summarize, the main attributes you might look for in a project manager are:

- Good people management and interpersonal skills
- Good communication skills
- The ability to plan and think ahead
- At least basic financial skills
- The ability to juggle many things at once
- The discipline to check and follow things through
- Good time management
- Good meetings organization and control
- Motivation, both personal and the ability to motivate others
- Enthusiasm.

These are not expressed in jargon or scientific terms, but they are all skills that any manager will recognize. Most are just good management practice. It is how they are brought together in the project situation that makes a *good* project manager.

THE PROJECT TEAM

The project team will be led by the project manager (see Chapter 3) who should also be an integral member of the team.

The temporary nature of the project group means that the team must quickly learn to work together, there is no time for interpersonal relationships to develop into a static state as is the situation in normal line management.

The team must quickly learn to work together

It would be an ideal situation for any project manager if he or she could analyse the needs of any project and then select the best team from individuals with the required knowledge experience and expertise. Sadly this is a most unlikely situation! It is most often the case that the members of a project team are not selected by the project manager or the client who commissions the project. The manager may be brought in to manage an existing team, or within a company the team may consist of the available personnel from the required disciplines.

Whatever the real situation, it is still worthwhile considering the 'ideal' team before we go on to see how we can make the best use of the team we have. It is not, however, quite that simple – there is no one ideal for a project team! Successful teams are as diverse as the projects they work. However there are certain key players and attributes which are common.

The project team should be as large or as small as the project requires. There is no point in bringing in more people than are needed – they will feel useless or cause mischief. It is up to the project manager to make sure that all who need to know are informed of what is going on – but they do not necessarily all need to be team members.

The team may also change as the project progresses – at different times different skills are required. As well as bringing additional team members on board if they are needed, others may be co-opted for specific tasks.

WHAT MAKES A 'GOOD' TEAM?

One fact in favour of the development of the project team is that human beings are naturally gregarious; they have a natural desire to seek the companionship of other human beings. Although social experiences and personal desires may lead some to be more individualistic than others, most people are willing to act cooperatively with at least one small reference group and usually more than one. The work group is frequently one of the most psychologically relevant groups for this cooperation.

SELECTING THE TEAM

If you are given the opportunity to bring together a team to undertake a project you should go through the following process:

1. List the main areas of activity which the project requires. You might choose to involve the customer (internal or external) in this process, especially if the project covers some areas you are unfamiliar with.
2. List all the possible team members who could undertake the task. This should include those who have the experience and expertise and possibly some who may not have all the experience you prefer but who have the ability to learn or adapt to the task and have other useful skills.
3. For everyone on the list rank them in terms of expertise, acceptability to the customer and track record in priority areas (for example, delivery on time, conformance to specification or cost). For example if the project is very cost sensitive you might prefer to use a cheaper supplier who takes longer than another.
4. Check possible team members' availability for the project duration.
5. Considering all the points above draw up a preferred list of team members.
6. From previous experience decide what the probability is of this group being able to form a good team (that is, work well together and be supportive to the project's needs). If this shows up any potential problems look for an alternative person to cover this role. This may mean including someone who needs more coaching or training in the job, but whose other attributes will contribute to the success of the project.

7. Discuss the project with each individual and find out if they are willing to be part of the project team. At this stage I use my discretion as to whether or not I divulge who else is being approached. This may be advantageous, but it is no good getting someone to agree to join on the suggestion that others are taking part if they have not already made a commitment.

BUILDING A TEAM

BRINGING THE TEAM TOGETHER

As far as possible the team members should be identified at the outset and involved in the planning stage. This will ensure that:

■ Their experience is used to aid successful planning
■ They will 'own' the parts of the plan they have to execute
■ They will feel part of the team.

Bringing the team together at an early stage may not be easy – but its value will far outweigh the difficulties.

Once the team has been selected, then the project manager has to provide the best environment for the team to learn to work together as quickly and efficiently as possible.

The team grouping can make a considerable contribution to the success in achieving objectives; and when objectives are achieved this reinforces the feelings of security and belonging and so can maximize contribution and cooperation. In other words, 'nothing breeds success like success'. If a team can achieve success early in its formation this will enhance the performance. The performance of the team will directly result in the success or otherwise of the project. Therefore the earliest stages in setting up and building the team can be crucial to the success of the project.

Much has been written about team building and I do not propose to go into the topic in any detail here. Suffice it to say that successful projects are executed by good teams, not a group of individuals.

> Bringing the team together at an early stage may not be easy – but its value will far outweigh the difficulties and the performance of the team will directly result in the success or otherwise of the project

THE DEVELOPING GROUP

A group is dynamic and during the progress of the project it will change. As it takes time for the group to develop into an effective team, the earlier they start working together the better. This process of working together can stagnate or even go into reverse, so it is not something which the project manager can set up once and for all. It must be worked at throughout the life of the project. Once the team has reached full effectiveness, however, it is fairly resistant to minor factors affecting it.

TRAINING NEEDS

It is not unreasonable to think that if you select your team carefully there will be no training need. This is most unlikely. The likelihood of bringing together a team all totally competent in all the technical requirements is not high, although possible. Even if you believe this to be true, it is still worth checking the abilities of your team. It can be done simply by drawing up a skills matrix. Figure 4.1 shows an example.

Skill	John	Chris	Angela	Mike	Julia
Accounting	na	na	na	na	R/P
Design	na	R/Y	na	R/Y	na
Surveying	R/Y	na	na	R/P	na
Construction	na	R/Y	na	R/Y	na
Legal	na	na	R/Y	na	na

Key

R = required
Y = skill good

P = skill needs some training
N = not competent
na = not applicable

FIGURE 4.1: Simplified skills matrix

Obviously this figure is a simplification, but it shows easily that there is some training required for Julia in accounting as she is the only team member responsible for this, and although Mike needs some training in surveying, this is mainly John's role and so that is not essential. You can produce a much more detailed matrix and subdivide training required into varying degrees of need or urgency.

Technical skills are a part of the training requirement, but building the team should also be considered. Few projects have the budget to do this on a grand scale or have the time to invest in long activities. However, it is valuable and the sooner the team are working together, the quicker good results will show.

The sooner the team are working together, the quicker good results will show

One way of tackling this is to have regular team meetings during the set up and planning stages early in the project. The meetings must have a definite objective, and within that it is possible to build in activities or discussion which will encourage the team to work together and build their relationships.

Meetings which have no real purpose and outcome are a waste of time and irritate the participants. They must also be well managed. If you are a project manager and need help with managing meetings there are a number of good videos and self study packages available on this subject.

ACCOUNTABILITY

Because most project teams will include individuals from different levels and different functions of the departments and companies involved in the project, there is no obvious hierarchy in the project team. For the project to run smoothly it will be necessary to establish some accountability within the team. This does *not* mean a hierarchical reporting structure. It means that each member of the team knows what he or she is responsible for and be empowered to carry this out. This will mean investing each team member with the authority to carry out certain tasks and make certain decisions without referring to the project manager. If the planning stage has been agreed by the team those who have to carry out the tasks will own them and be willing to put in the necessary effort to achieve their objectives. Again, this should not preclude discussion and sharing of ideas and problems. If the team is working well together, members will be willing to share and ask for advice.

> Each member of the team knows what he or she is responsible for and empowered to carry this out

In successful projects the project manager will provide the leadership necessary to develop a manageable team and the organization must support his or her role. A company with a policy of participation will enable the project team to achieve good results. This includes sharing the problems as well as the successes, carrying out fair analyses of why things go wrong and sharing the implementation of the solutions. The Land Rover case is a good example of this philosophy.

> A company with a policy of participation will enable the project team to achieve good results. This includes sharing the problems as well as the successes

This may require major changes within many organizations, and some project teams will not have the advantage of working in organizations or for clients with true open management. However, by carrying out this philosophy within the team and ensuring that the team members are empowered as well as accountable they have a good chance of making up for some of these shortcomings.

COMMUNICATION

A part of the philosophy described in the last section is one of open communication. The development of trust will encourage open communication. I have frequently used the term 'sharing' and this requires communication. The project manager can help to develop this and resolve communication problems in a number of ways.

The signs that a manager can be on the lookout for are, for example, team members at a project meeting who do not pay attention to each other, show a lack of respect for the views of others or members pre-occupied with personal objectives. Resolving these problems can be tackled by good interpersonal communication between the manager and individuals and through open discussion among team members. It is up to the project manager to decide which is the best method for tackling any issue or potential issue, but by good monitoring they should not reach crisis proportions before they are spotted and dealt with.

> One of the most common causes of dissent within a group is misunderstanding or lack of factual information

One of the most common causes of dissent within a group is misunderstanding or lack of factual information. Where information does not exist rumour may take its place. Where only half a story is available the rest is filled in by guesswork. Both these situations could easily be avoided by good communication. Every project should have a formal communication system. In small projects with a small team in one location this can easily be accomplished. With large teams, geographically widespread it appears to be more difficult – but with modern technology there is no need for it to be so.

At the outset of the project methods of communication should be agreed upon. They should then be monitored and amended as necessary. A simple system for communication which can be adapted for small or large projects could be designed. The checklist below suggests ideas which you can adapt to your needs.

Communications checklist

Weekly meetings at each activity group level.
Simple bullet point minutes produced on the spot and faxed or e-mailed to heads of all other activity groups.
Monthly meetings of activity group leaders.
Simple bullet point minutes produced on the spot with actions highlighted.
Shared with all activity group members at the weekly meetings.
Strategic decisions from company level handed down to project manager.

> Project manager shares with activity group leaders at
> monthly meetings; if more urgent calls special meeting
> or faxes/e-mails to all activity group leaders immediately.
> At all meetings (activity group and group leaders) actions
> from last meeting reviewed.
> Formal letters and memos only written when there are
> either contractual or legal implications or parties outside
> the project team involved.
> Copies of all meeting notes are kept in a central file in
> each project office.
> For actions agreed outside the regular meetings similar
> brief notes are written, shared and filed.

This ensures that:

- All actions from meetings are noted and agreed
- Actions are monitored
- All team members are informed of all relevant information
- Minimum time is taken in writing formal letters and memos.

COMPETENCIES

In many organizations and professions the ability of individuals to
carry out their job is expressed as competencies. Many specific jobs
have industry standards or competencies available. These can assist a
manager in assessing the ability of an individual to carry out a
specific task. Project management is not a precise science and in this
chapter we have looked at the various skills which make a good
project manager and considered how we can put together and build
a team with desirable skills.

To help managers who are considering more advanced training
for project management there is a document available which
describes competencies for project management. It is available from
the Association for Project Management (the address is given in
Further useful information at the end of the book).

SESSION 4 – EXERCISES WITH YOUR TEAM

OVERVIEW

The following exercises will enable your team to look more closely
at the skills within the team and then establish where there are skill
gaps and training needs.

They will then go on to consider the value of good

communications during the project and look at ways in which their own communications can be improved.

EQUIPMENT AND MATERIALS

Flip chart, notepaper and pens.

PREPARATION

Before you begin you should look back at Exercise 3.2 where you drew up a list of management skills. Write this out or produce your original charts.

Also make a note of the key areas from this chapter which you want to pass on to your team. This will form the introduction to this session. Make a note and write out on a chart the key project skills you think the team should have.

For Exercise 4.2 draw up a simple skills matrix as shown in Figure 4.1 but without any skills. Add the names of your team to it.

For Exercise 4.3 take the communications checklist shown earlier in this chapter and copy it on to a flip chart.

METHOD

Discussion and brainstorming.

TIME

Exercise 4.1 will take about 20 minutes. Exercise 4.2 will take 10–15 minutes brainstorming then discussion of about 15–20 minutes. Exercise 4.3 will take about 20 minutes.

Exercise 4.1

Steps
1. Describe the key points that you have learned from this chapter.
2. Show the list of key skills you have drawn up.
3. Ask the team to add any further skills they think are important. You can then use this list in Exercise 4.2.

Exercise 4.2

Steps
1. Consider a project you are likely to be working on or would like to undertake. Do not choose an existing or past project.

2. Look at the list of team members on the skills matrix you have already drawn up and add any you think may join the team for this project.
3. Look back at the criteria for a team working well together. What, if any, additional information would help you in making an effective team? Brainstorm this.
4. Add the required skills to your matrix.
5. You may choose to discuss the team's training needs in broad terms at this stage, or you may prefer to do this on a one-to-one basis later.

SUMMARY

THE HUMAN SIDE OF PROJECTS
Project teams are groups of humans. Their individual needs and understanding of their roles are essential to the good functioning of the project.

THE PROJECT MANAGER
Good project managers are good people managers. The project manager must be given the authority to manage, but also requires certain personal and personnel skills.

THE PROJECT TEAM
Project teams are often temporary and so must quickly learn to work together. Good teams should be selected for their technical skills, personal skills and ability to work together.

When selecting the team the manager should find out about:

- Preferred styles
- Technical skills
- Proven track record
- Availability
- Good 'team' skills
- Willingness to participate in the particular project.

The quicker a team is built into a good working unit, the more successful the project will be. This can be helped by ensuring early successes and planning to involve the team as early in the process as possible so that they 'own' their work. The project manager can assist the building of the team and should also monitor its progress as a team, as well as the work it performs. The team will develop and change as the project progresses.

Skills can be developed through training and team building activities.

ACCOUNTABILITY

Team members must know what they are responsible for and they should be empowered to carry out their responsibilities.

COMMUNICATION

Good communication is essential to project success.

Formal systems should be set up but they should be simple and not time consuming. Informal systems also have a value but to avoid rumour and misinformation the formal systems need to be effective.

CHAPTER 5

*T*HE PROJECT MANAGEMENT TRIANGLE

KEY LEARNING POINTS

- Understand the meaning of the three elements of quality, cost and time
- Understand the requirements needed to balance the three elements
- Understand the effects of changing priorities

QUALITY

There are many definitions of quality but it must be remembered that quality does not mean 'luxury' or 'up market' – these are subjective descriptions. The definitions of quality which I prefer are those used by engineers or manufacturers, that is:

- Fitness for purpose
- Zero defects
- Conformance to specification.

All of these would be suitable for describing the purpose of *quality* in a project management sense. To measure the outcomes of the project, the specification must be set and agreed at the beginning. The success of the project in quality terms will depend upon it meeting these specifications.

COST

In project management terms this is the *project cost* – and that is usually the final cost. The budget is the figure you set out with; that is, what you have available to spend or what you are wanting to spend on the project. But the real cost is what you actually spend when the project is complete. We will consider costs in more detail in Chapters 9 and 13.

TIME

Again, in project management terms this is the actual time taken to complete the project. When planning a project you can start with a required end date and work back to the present, putting in enough resources to complete on time. Alternatively, you can plan all your tasks, allocate the required time and fit these in with available resources. This will produce a given end date. In reality most projects are a compromise of these and during the progress of the project there will be fluctuations in timings even if the end date remains the same.

We will explore time and project schedules further in Chapters 7 and 11.

WHY A TRIANGLE?

Any three-part entity is an interesting balance. If you have three people on a committee they will rarely all agree – it is often a two versus one situation and so balances and compromises may have to be made for the sake of harmony. If you look at a three-legged stool, it is very firm unless you take one leg away!

The project management triangle is not quite as sensitive as a three-legged stool – but it will certainly work best when all three elements are in balance or harmony. The three elements are normally shown as a triangle because all are interdependent and equally valuable. You will see in Figure 5.1 that this has been shown as an equilateral triangle. This is the ideal – no one element being more important than either of the others. But this is rarely the case in reality. Even if a project starts with all being of equal importance, this may change during the life of the project. The following example illustrates this:

The project management triangle will certainly work best when all three elements are in balance or harmony

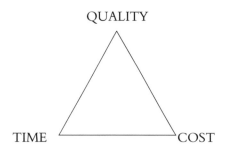

FIGURE 5.1: The project management triangle

An advertising campaign for a new product is planned. The product is to be launched in October and the campaign is to run from one month prior to the launch to Christmas. A budget is agreed and the specification for the products (television commercials, posters, magazine and newspaper copy) is agreed to certain standards of production. The product is a high-value, luxury product aimed at an A/B level audience, so the advertising must reflect this.

Planning starts in December of the previous year, giving nine months to the campaign launch, 10 months to the product launch.

The quality/cost/time factors are agreed and in balance.

In February, it is learned that a major competitor is launching a similar product in September – one month before ours. What shall we do? The options are:

1. Launch advertising early but keep product on schedule
2. Launch product and advertising early
3. Keep to original plans and rely on brand loyalty and a better quality product to win over.

Option three was ruled out as too risky. Option two was not possible due to lead times for prototype trials and completion of the production line. One was the preferred option – at least it would let customers know what was coming and enable advance orders to be taken by the time the rival product was launched.

To achieve this, two major changes to the triangle were essential:

1. Timescales had to be shortened.
2. The specification for the advertising was to be changed.

To achieve this, more resources were essential and additional advertising time/space had to be purchased.

So, in our example, to change time and quality (or specification), costs had to be altered. This kept the project in balance although priorities had been altered, that is, it was agreed that more cost would be made available because time was the first priority now and a new specification was the next priority.

It is rarely possible to make major changes to one of the elements without affecting at least one, if not both, of the others. These changes may be caused by factors beyond the control of the project team – as in our advertising example – or they may be as the result of team actions, but changes are not necessarily problems. If things go well in a project which has plenty of spare (or *float*) time built in, this would mean earlier delivery or enable the project manager to reduce resources and still deliver on time at a lower cost.

It is up to the customer and project manager to agree the initial targets for quality, cost and time. The project manager must agree with his or her team how these will be met within the constraints of the project brief. Once this has been done, day to day fluctuations and problems should be controlled by the project manager, but major changes (especially those beyond the control of the project team) may have to be discussed with the client and new priorities agreed. The questions to be asked are:

- If *quality* is the priority, do we need more resources, that is, can we put in more cost, or do we lengthen the project?
- If *cost* is the priority, can we reschedule or change our objectives?
- If *time* is the priority, can we add more resources, that is, cost, or alter our objectives?

Whatever the question, decide and agree the priority, then use the balance between the other two to revise plans accordingly.

SESSION 5 – EXERCISE WITH YOUR TEAM

OVERVIEW

The outcomes of the following exercise will vary depending on the projects chosen and your detailed knowledge of them. It will work best if at least one member of your team knows the project you choose to discuss well enough to understand any constraints or possibilities for change which existed at the time.

It is rarely possible to make major changes to one of the elements without affecting at least one, if not both, of the others

---

EQUIPMENT AND MATERIALS

You will require a room for your meeting, laid out so all participants can see each other and the flip chart. You will also need a flip chart and the outcomes of the exercises from Chapter 3.

PREPARATION

Look back at Chapter 3, Exercise 3.1, for the list of project successes and failures. Re-write the list of factors for failure on a flip chart.

METHOD

The method is discussion and brainstorming.

TIME

The total time for this exercise will be about 60–80 minutes, depending on how long you allow for discussion.

Exercise 5.1

Steps

1. Go through the list of factors for failure from Exercise 3.1 one by one with your team. For all the factors listed note by the side whether the failure was in quality, cost or time.
2. Pick at least one marked 'quality' and discuss whether revising priorities and therefore time/cost issues would have helped. If not, why not?
3. Repeat point 2 for cost.
4. Repeat point 2 for time.
5. Looking at your answers to points 2, 3 and 4 above, on balance, would revising priorities have helped? If not, why is this so and what other factors would we need to take into account?

COMMENT

If your outcomes for this exercise do *not* show a case for revising priorities you should consider, 'Why is this?' Unless the parameters are unrealistic (for example, drastically reduced time with exactly the same budget while increasing expected outcomes) there should be some room for revising the priorities and bringing the project back into balance.

This re-balancing is made easier by planning in contingencies for change. We will look at this idea in the chapters on planning. It can also be affected by how you handle changes and potential changes. We will explore this further in the chapters on monitoring and control.

SUMMARY

Projects can only be measured objectively if the objectives were clearly set at the outset. Subjective measurement of ill-defined projects is not scientific; it is sometimes the only way to judge success or failure if the project specification was not clear – but any conclusions you draw from these judgements will also be subjective and, therefore, not scientific.

Quality, cost and time are the three main elements of project management and are seen as a triangle, with each being interdependent. To manage the project successfully, these targets must be set at the planning stage and kept in balance during the duration of the project. Changes to one will affect the others, so all three will need to be considered to maintain the balance.

CHAPTER 6

WHY PLAN AHEAD?

KEY LEARNING POINTS

- ■ Understand the value of planning
- ■ Know how to set project objectives
- ■ Understand the meaning and value of project strategies
- ■ Describe considerations necessary when planning a project
- ■ Know the main stages of planning and the phases of a project
- ■ Know how the phases influence project costs
- ■ Know what constraints may affect projects

DOES IT REQUIRE A PLAN?

Some projects are so simple that either there is only one way to do them, that is, it does not matter how you do them because the outcomes will always be the same, or there are not enough different tasks and resources to make it worthwhile.

As a simple example, going back to the idea of planning a journey we described in Chapter 2, if the journey is a brief one with only one possible method of transport it is hardly worth planning. However, if it is a round the world tour for 20 people, a plan is essential! If a project involves a variety of tasks spread over a period

If a project involves a variety of tasks spread over a period of time and involves more than one resource it is worth considering a plan

of time and involves more than one resource it is worth considering a plan. As more time, more tasks and more resources are added, planning becomes more important. The complexity of tasks and resources is probably more important than the length of time. A simple task spread over a long period of time will not necessarily require planning, but many different tasks carried out by a variety of resources over a short period may.

There is no scientific or exact measure of when a formal planning process becomes necessary, but a useful guideline is to begin by answering these five questions:

1. How will the success or failure of the project be judged?
2. How can I monitor and control the project?
3. How will I ensure that all team members know their responsibilities and targets?
4. How will I ensure that all resources are available when and where I need them?
5. How can I take account of changes during the life of the project?

For a successful project, the project objectives must be clear and must be agreed

If you do not know the answer to question 1, then the project objectives are not clear. For a successful project these must be agreed. If the answers to questions 2–5 are that you do not know or are even partly unsure then there is a clear requirement for a project plan.

The planning stage is very important, it is through the plan that problems (actual and potential) can be identified. This will enable you to develop strategies to handle these.

HOW WILL IT HELP?

Planning takes time and effort, so there is a temptation to cut down on the planning and get on with the project. This is a short-sighted approach. Time you save at the outset by 'getting on with the project' is likely to be wasted later in activities to remedy early mistakes.

QUALITY

If you do not set objectives how will you know when or whether you have achieved anything? These objectives must also be sensible and achievable. Hadrian's Wall gives us an interesting example of what might at first appear to be good planning but in fact was not a success in all aspects:

The wall was planned to have gateways with 'milecastles' for defence built on one side of the wall at intervals of one mile. A mile was a reasonable distance for a foot soldier to run so this seemed a sensible design.

The design criteria had to be followed faithfully by the builders. Presumably the design criteria for the wall were written in Rome, or at least by someone who had never visited the site and did not realize that the wall was to be built across mountainous country.

The result is that some of the milecastles are built even where there are near precipitous drops outside the gates, making them useless. The men building the wall built a gate every mile whether it was of any use or not!

Again, this presents a number of interesting lessons. Was the design wrong or were the builders incompetent? Neither is entirely true – the objectives had not been thoroughly researched and so were not sensible or realistic. We can safely assume that the builders did not have the authority or expertise to question the design. Whatever the reason, the product may have conformed to specification but the specification was not well planned.

COST

Experience shows that there are far fewer overruns in cost and time if the cost and time estimates are accurate in the first place. This may involve investing some time and cost in a proper upfront plan or feasibility study. This could cost three to five per cent of the total project cost, but it is better than abandoning a project halfway through and wasting *all* the cost because you have run out of budget.

The Downey Report looking into instances of cancelled aeronautical projects with the Ministry of Defence, among other things indicated the wisdom of spending a limited amount of money on feasibility studies on a project before committing the bulk of the budget. When the feasibility study comes out as negative, expenditure will be limited; if positive, the planning involved will help the subsequent progress of the project.

The Downey Report described four main phases or subdivisions. It indicated approximate percentages of the nominal project cost which could be expected to be spent on each phase. The graph in Figure 6.1 shows their findings.

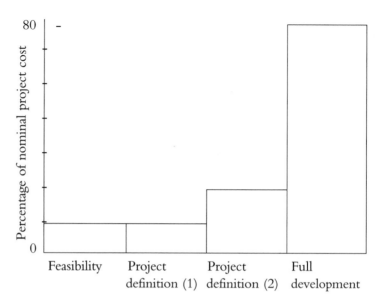

FIGURE 6.1: Relative influence of typical project phases on total project cost

TIME

Forward planning can also save time later. The following example may seem simplistic but it shows the value of planning even on apparently simple projects:

A small software company was writing a new piece of software. They had undergone the market research, defined the objectives for the program and planned the design, programming and testing phases into their manpower resource chart. It would be ready to launch at the next computer show. They had even thought of writing a manual for users and the main program designer agreed to begin this once the overall structure and key elements of the program were at the Beta test (i.e. second major test) stage.

At the appropriate stage, writing of the manual began. They were now six weeks from launch. When the bulk of the writing was complete (four weeks later) they approached a graphics studio to do a layout. Producing visuals for client approval would take a week but all their graphics people were currently busy with projects and could not start this for at least a week. Layout (assuming the designs were acceptable) would take a further two weeks, then add another week for checking and corrections if all went well. That only left one week for printing and that was the week their usual printer was on shut down. What could they do? There were a number of solutions, all involving paying overtime or going to alternative suppliers whom they did not know, so were unsure of their reliability.

There are lessons here in having a number of sources of supply – but the most important one is that if they had planned ahead properly and in detail they could have:

1. Got the design stage under way before writing was complete, so saving overall time.
2 Booked the designers they required to be available when needed.
3. Approached the printer to find out their schedules and agreed to deliver the artwork in time to get it printed before their shut down.

WHAT IS THE PROJECT PLAN?

The project plan is a management document which should specify:

- Objectives
- Policies
- Tactics
- Products.

It should cover what we must do and when we must do it. On the basis of this project plan the time and cost commitments can be made. There are various structured techniques for planning which identify the sequence and relationship of different stages of a project. We will look at these in more detail in Chapters 7 and 8. A good plan will provide the indications of performance against which programmes can be checked. These are the objectives, milestones and terms of reference.

OBJECTIVES AND STRATEGIES

Much has been written and discussed about the setting of objectives, but it is so important to the planning stage of your project that the key points will be summarized here.

To enable you to measure your success objectively, you must have objectives to measure against. These must be specific and measurable. A project objective must specify in as precise detail as possible and should state:

- What the activity is
- Methods or techniques which must be applied
- Details of the outcomes to be measured
- Whose responsibility it is.

Let us look at a simple example. If you were to be asked to 'build a wall' would you know what is expected of you? It is a bit vague and if you asked six different people you would probably get six different plans. You need to specify height, length, materials, costs, timescales, location and so on, that is you need to set specific measurable objectives. We will develop this example in the exercise session at the end of this chapter.

Given a clear specification of requirements and techniques to be used you can be sure of getting what you want.

There are four key principles involved in formulating an objective. They can be described as shown in Figure 6.2.

Principle	Example	Elements
Details of required end product	Length and height of wall, materials to be used	Targets
Standards to be attained	Time and cost constraints; standard of finish	Performance criteria
Methods to be used	Number of people and other resources required	Preferred execution strategies
Overriding priorities	Use of specialist bricks regardless of expense	Priorities

FIGURE 6.2: Four key principles involved in formulating an objective

Let us look at each of these in more detail.

TARGETS

If you aim at nothing you're sure to hit it.

You must be able to specify and control your projects much more precisely than this! You must specify targets, identifying stages in the progress of the project as well as the end point.

You need to keep track during the progress of the project, not just at the end. Targets should include quantifiable details such as cost and time.

PERFORMANCE CRITERIA

There are the standards which are set for each target area to ensure the quality of performance in managing the project. Just getting something done is not enough, we must have completed it to the standard set – that is, quality as well as cost and time.

> Just getting something done is not enough, we must have completed it to the standard set – that is, quality as well as cost and time

PREFERRED EXECUTION STRATEGIES

These will specify any particular methods to be used or special operational decisions. It could cover topics such as:

- Project personnel – in-house or sub-contract?
- Equipment – existing or new?
- Particular type of materials.

These may need to be set at the planning stage to ensure consistency and fit with company policy or other criteria. In the project plan reasons should be stated so that all the team understand the reasons for the decision.

PRIORITIES

We may need to give riders to some of the targets such as 'regardless of costs' for the use of a specific material. This will help the project manager prioritize their targets. Again, it is useful to give reasons for such decisions.

ACTIONS

At the detailed level of planning, objectives can be expressed in terms of specific outcomes (or actions) which must be carried out.

SETTING OBJECTIVES

An objective is 'something sought or aimed at'. The golden rules for any objective are that it is:

- Clear
- Unambiguous
- Appropriate
- Attainable
- Measurable.

Starting with the *overall objectives* for the project, ask yourself the following questions:

1. What are we trying to achieve?
2. What are the standards and criteria which must be met?
3. Are there any specific methods which must be applied?
4. What are the parameters within which it should be achieved?

For example, we are going to build a wall and these are the objectives:

1. Build a wall.
2. 20 metres long, 3 metres high, ½ metre thick. It must be vertical in a straight line and built to appropriate British Standard.
3. Materials – breeze block. Built by hand.
4. To be completed in 5 days.

These are fairly broad objectives, but they set the framework for you to work within and they give some vital information. For example, time is an important factor, so you will need to plan resources to meet this parameter.

By putting your various requirements *in* to the project you will be able to control it and get *out* the outcomes you need. These are summed up in the input and output diagram shown in Figure 6.3.

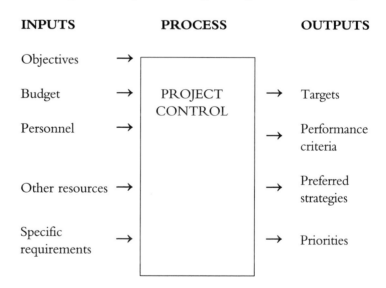

FIGURE 6.3: Summary of objectives and strategies

The more detailed objectives will then be set as the next step and alongside the confirmation of the detailed specification. So, for our 'wall building project' the specification might be:

Height
Length
Width
Materials
Foundations
Shape (vertical and horizontal)
Load bearing capacity, etc.

PLANNING STRUCTURE

The establishment of *overall objectives* is the initial stage in project planning. These will need to be broken down into more detailed levels and responsibilities. These are shown in the Figure 6.4.

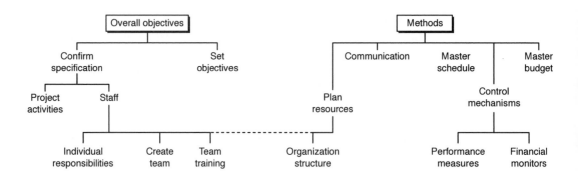

FIGURE 6.4: Considerations for planning structure

This structure plan can be used as a template for any project and you can use it to produce a checklist of considerations for a project plan. We have already considered the topics of *specification* and *setting objectives*. We also need to plan staff (resources) and break the project down into elements, then consider the methods of the project in detail. We will be looking at these in the following chapters.

PROJECT PHASES

Every project passes through a number of phases and this will influence how the project can be controlled. The principal phases can be considered as:

1. Project definition
2. Feasibility
3. Initial specification
4. Estimation
5. Proposal
6. Planning
7. Engineering design (if appropriate)
8. Implementation (including Purchase and Procurement)
9. Installation (if appropriate)
10. Commissioning
11. Run-up
12. Project review.

If you compare this list to the phases shown in Figure 6.1 you will see that we have expanded upon the four simple phases and given more detail. The next stage of detail will vary from project to project and you will need to draw up your own list of stages for each project you undertake. However, this list will serve as a useful guide and starting point.

Subdividing the project into phases will help you to have a controllable framework for each project and will enable you to write the objectives and strategies with terms of reference to guide towards the successful completion of the project.

The definition and feasibility phases are particularly important as part of the planning as they will establish whether or not a project under consideration is viable. Great care, systematic research and objective decision making must be practised during this phase as decisions made here will establish the structure and guidelines for the complete project.

Subdividing the project into phases will help you to have a controllable framework for each project

PROJECT CONSTRAINTS

There are likely to be constraints on any project. They will differ from project to project depending on the priorities, pressures and problems, but require initial analysis during the early definition phases of the project. If constraints are not fully analysed at the outset they will become a recurrent theme during the project causing blocks, restrictions, delays and frustrations and could lead to a second rate project. Where the constraints are known at the outset of detailed design the resultant design and planning will minimize potential negative effects, thus making the best use of the resources available.

The major constraints on a project can be grouped under four headings:

There are likely to be constraints on any project:
■ **business**
■ **economic**
■ **environmental**
■ **technical**

- *Business constraints:*
  - Government or legal requirements
  - Business objectives
  - Management directives.
- *Economic constraints*:
  - Cost
  - Need to give the project justification.
- *Environmental constraints*:
  - Skills and resources available
  - Communications
  - Security requirements
  - Procedures and methodologies
  - Physical circumstances.
- *Technical constraints*:
  - Company/industry technical standards and limitations
  - Equipment policy.

SESSION 6 – EXERCISES WITH YOUR TEAM

OVERVIEW

Exercise 6.1 will help your team to understand the need for project planning and give them an opportunity to air their own views on the subject. Exercise 6.2 will then show them how to set objectives.

EQUIPMENT AND MATERIALS

For each exercise you will require a room for discussion with your team. You will also need a flip chart and the team will need paper and pens.

PREPARATION

You will need to prepare a list of reasons why planning is important. Do this by making notes from this chapter, especially the summary.

For Exercise 6.2 you will require a flip chart showing the 'Golden rules of objectives' (see step 4 below).

TIME

Exercise 6.1 should take 5–10 minutes' brainstorming, plus 15–20 minutes' discussion. Exercise 6.2 should take about 20–30 minutes.

Exercise 6.1

Steps

1. Brainstorm with the team why you think planning is important.
2. When you have done this for 5–10 minutes, compare this with your own list. Discuss with the group any differences and encourage them to air their own views on the value of planning.
3. From the discussion and the two lists try to reach agreement on the main reasons why they *should* plan their projects. Note these on a flip chart.
4. Ask one or two team members to prepare a list entitled 'Why we should plan projects' as a handout to go into everyone's training folders.

Exercise 6.2

Steps

1. With little preamble and no detailed explanation, ask your team (each member individually) to write down their response to the following instruction: 'Give the steps involved in building a wall from initial planning to completion'.
2. Go round the group and ask for their responses. Chances are you will have nearly as many answers as people!
3. Discuss why there is such a variety of responses. They should realize that the task you set was too vague. It needed specific objectives.
4. Draw out by discussion if you have time, or just give them if time is short, the list of golden rules. That is, objectives must be:
   – Clear
   – Unambiguous
   – Appropriate
   – Attainable
   – Measurable.
5. Ask them to come up with a list of objectives for the wall building exercise.
6. Discuss their answers and compare them with the list of golden rules.

SUMMARY

WHY PLAN?

Any project with a variety of activities and resources can benefit from a project plan. The more complex the project, the more essential a plan becomes.

A good project plan may take up time initially and therefore incur some costs, but it will save cost, time and other mistakes during the process of the project. It will enable accurate monitoring and control of the project. The earliest stages are the least expensive, but have the greatest effect on eventual costs. In extreme cases the plan may even show that the project is not viable and provide the data for a decision to abort before too much cost has been incurred.

Planning will:

- Tell you *what* you have to do *when*
- Show what resources are needed when
- Show what budget is required for the project
- Help you to decide if the project is feasible or not
- Enable you to monitor and control your project
- Help to avoid frustrations brought about by unexpected occurrences
- Enable you to bring the project in on *time* to *cost* and at the required *quality*.

OBJECTIVES AND TARGETS

To ensure success the project should have clear objectives which can be measured. The targets and strategies for achieving these should also be written into the project plan and the performance criteria, priorities and actions required explained.

In writing clear and accurate objectives you need to be specific about at least six key points:

- What the activity is
- Level of responsibility and ownership for budget
- Necessary details to be achieved
- Standards and criteria to be met
- Particular methods which must be applied
- Functional areas or contractors who will be expected to provide resources for the teams.

THE GOLDEN RULES OF OBJECTIVES

Objectives must be:

- Clear

- Unambiguous
- Appropriate
- Attainable
- Measurable.

CONSTRAINTS

All projects are subject to constraints, some within and some beyond the control of the project manager or the organization. Although at first these may appear to have a negative effect on the project they can sometimes be of value and may be used to assist the planning and execution of the project.

STRUCTURE AND HIERARCHY

The project plan is not one simple action or series of activities. Every project is made up of a number of stages or phases and each of these will have particular considerations. The overall objectives will need to be broken down into more detailed objectives for each of these stages of the project.

The project also has a hierarchical structure and each level in this hierarchy requires different levels of detail in the planning and the information it requires for monitoring and control later on.

CHAPTER 7

PRODUCING A PROJECT PLAN 1: TIME

KEY LEARNING POINTS

■ Know how to begin planning and to focus on project
  objectives
■ Know the three principles of planning and how to gather
  together the relevant data for a plan
■ Know the steps required to draw up a project plan
■ Be able to recognize three different types of project plans

PRINCIPLES OF PLANNING

One problem is that project plans are usually based on
incomplete information. The planning, then, may not be perfect,
but detailed planning will at least restrict the number of
unexpected difficulties.

One problem is that project
plans are usually based on
incomplete information

Our first principle is to, *Gather together all available data at the
time*. We saw how important this is when we considered project
failures in Chapter 2. But this principle accepts that changes take
place during the progress of the project – new data becomes
available, unexpected things happen, the parameters may even

change. So to be successful these changes can be put into the plan and it can be adapted accordingly.

Our second principle is that, *Plans must be flexible working tools – not tablets of stone*. Your project plan is only a means to an end. It is intended to help you manage your project. There is no right or wrong technique, some may suit your method of working better than others; others may suit the particular project in hand better.

Our third principle is to, *Choose the most appropriate technique for you, your team and your project*. You will be able to do this when you have learned more about the different techniques available.

To produce a good chart or plan, whether manually or by computer, it will be helpful if you work through a number of stages. These stages establish:

- What activities are to be done
- What activities depend on each other
- How long they will take
- When they have to be done
- Who has to do them.

You will be able to do this if you work through the six key steps described here.

KEY STEPS OF PLANNING

Like any big task, project planning is easier if you break it down into small steps. This chapter concentrates on producing a project plan which will show *time* and *resources*. It will enable you to see how long the project will take and in what order things must be done. At the end of this process you will end up with:

- All the activities you have to perform in the correct order
- Activities dependent on each other in the correct order
- The earliest and latest start and finish time for each activity
- The resources for each activity listed
- The *critical path* for your project highlighted.

Costs can be added later.

Exercise 7.1 later in this chapter will use a simple example (making a cup of tea) to take you through the six steps described here.

Like any big task, project planning is easier if you break it down into small steps

STEP 1: ACTIVITIES AND CHUNKING

For any project, start by making a list and describing every single activity which needs to take place. It is helpful to do this using separate sheets of paper or cards for each one. This will enable you to add extra information to them later and to move them around into different sequences.

In more complex projects it is easier if you start by breaking the whole project down into small units or *chunks*; (these could also be referred to as *activity packages*). So for this method you will start by listing the main chunks of your project. Then later on you can take each chunk and describe each activity which comprises that chunk. Your cards or pages could look like those shown in Figure 7.1.

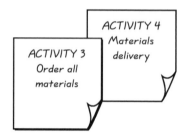

FIGURE 7.1: Activities

STEP 2: ADDING DETAIL

For each activity you can add:

- What resources that activity requires (number of people or actual names if you have them)
- How long it will take.

Your sheets might now look like those in Figure 7.2.

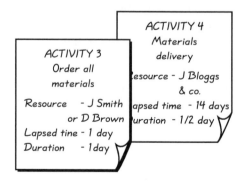

FIGURE 7.2: Activities detail

STEP 3: GROUPING AND SEQUENCING

Next sort all the activities into a logical sequence. To do this take each one and decide:

- What do you need to do now?
- What must you do before that?
- What can be done after that?
- What can be done at the same time?

It may help if you lay your sheets out or pin them to a board. They could then look like those in Figure 7.3. You will see that they are not in the sequence in which you wrote them; they are now in the order in which they must be carried out.

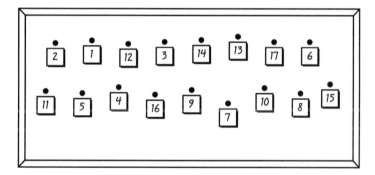

FIGURE 7.3: Activities and dependencies

If you have already divided your project into chunks, then tackle steps 2 and 3 for each chunk one at a time. If the project did not seem to be complex at first, you probably did not think it needed *chunking*, but if you now find that it contains a lot of activities it may help to group them at this stage. First group any activities which form *natural groupings*, then sort your groups and activities into a sequence. This step is how you build up your activity packages.

You have now started to work out the *dependencies* of the activities and have the basis of your network. However, you may not yet have taken your resourcing into account.

STEP 4: RESOURCING AND DEPENDENCIES

If you look at the example of building a wall you can see that you have some activities which could take place in parallel (that is, at the same time). For example, if 'Deliver materials' and 'Dig foundations' require different resources they can be done at the same time. The example given in Figure 7.4 uses two resources, B and C, and

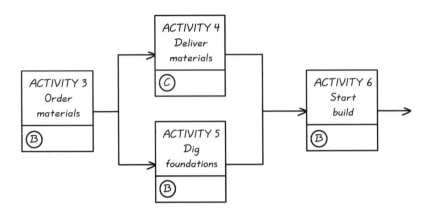

FIGURE 7.4: Activities with resources

we have linked them to show how two activities can be carried out in parallel.

For some activities which could theoretically happen in parallel, you may find that you are not able to do this in reality because they require the same resource, and this resource cannot do two jobs at once. This means that these activities have to be done in sequence.

In the example given in Figure 7.5 'Mix mortar' and 'Lay bricks' could, in theory, be done at the same time, but as there is only B to do both, they cannot.

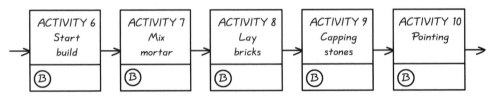

FIGURE 7.5: Further activities with resources

STEP 5: CALCULATING 'EARLIEST START' AND 'LATEST FINISH'

If you have not already done so, now is the time to put the time taken or *duration* of your activities into each sheet. This can be in hours/days/weeks or any unit you choose. It could look like Figure 7.6, where the chosen units are days.

If Activity 1 starts on day one and takes two days it will finish on day two. Activity 2 then starts on day three; it only takes one day so it finishes on day three. Activity 3 starts on day four, takes two days, so finishes on day five and so on. In this way you can work out

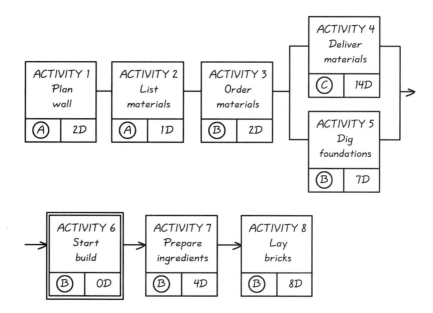

FIGURE 7.6: Durations for activities

the earliest date each activity can start and the latest time it can finish. Activity 6 has no duration, therefore it is a *milestone*.

STEP 6: ESTABLISHING THE 'CRITICAL PATH'

In Figure 7.7 we have added the earliest start (ES) date and latest finish (LF) date for each activity. The earliest start date is when all the preceding activities have finished and must allow enough time for this to happen. The latest finish is how late it can be completed so the next activity can begin on time.

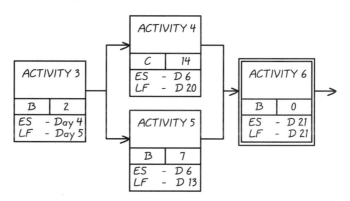

FIGURE 7.7: Durations with float

Sometimes activities have a *float*; that is, there is more time available to do them than they require. In Activity 5 in our example the earliest start is day six and latest finish is day 13. This gives a time of seven days, but the next activity's (Activity 6) earliest start is day 21. So, in fact, Activity 5 has a float of seven days. This is because Activity 6 cannot start until Activity 4 finishes, that is, Activity 6 is dependent on Activity 4, and that takes 14 days.

The *critical path* is made up of activities with *no float*. That is, their duration is exactly the same as the time available to do them. Any extra time required to do these activities will mean the project overruns its expected finish time.

The *critical path* is made up of activities with *no float*

It is possible to find more than one critical path on some projects, or, if you have a specified end date and you can complete the project before then, there may be no critical path! The chart we have drawn is an example of a type of *Critical Path Network* (CPN).

CHANGING THE CRITICAL PATH

If you plan shows that your end date is too late you can look at the resources to see if adding extra resources would help. For example, if you added another person to do Activity 7 in the example in Figure 7.6, this could be carried out in parallel with Activity 8, thus saving you two days. Obviously this is only possible with activities which can take place in parallel or when more resources can speed them up so, alternatively, you could add extra resources to one activity such as putting two people on Activity 8 (laying bricks) and so reducing this to four days.

NETWORKS

The project plan example we have just worked through has shown you how to produce a simple network. The benefits of this method are that it shows the sequence of events and dependencies visually in a simple graphical way. There are, however, variety of planning methods using different types of network diagram, Gantt charts or histograms. You are likely to see or use these in future and so need to recognize them and understand how they work.

Some of the networks which have been used in the past are less common now because the use of computer programs for producing project plans has superseded them. For this reason there are no detailed explanations of these types of network. Further detail in the use of computers is given in Chapter 14.

BASIC NETWORK STRUCTURE

Initial planning is very important

With all charts, initial planning is very important. You must:

1. Decide activities (either working forwards or backwards – whichever is easier).
2. Decide order of activities.
3. Decide which activities are dependent on which (ask 'what must be completed before this activity can start?').
4. Estimate times for activities

From this information a variety of network diagrams could be constructed.

PERT (PROGRAMME EVALUATION AND REVIEW TECHNIQUE)

This technique introduces a flexibility into estimating the completion time for activities, rather than relying on potentially subjective estimates in *Critical Path Method* (CPM).
PERT requires three estimates of time for each activity:

■ An optimistic estimate – where everything goes right without a hitch
■ A normal estimate
■ A pessimistic estimate – where everything that can go wrong, does go wrong!

Apart from this, the same basic networking format as we saw earlier is used.

The decision to use PERT instead of CPM will depend largely on:

■ The size of the project
■ The availability of a computer
■ Previous networking experience.

PERT is most likely to be used on larger scale projects. It is also the basis of most of the critical path charts which are used by computer project management techniques. For this reason it is more common than other types of critical path charts.

Many modern computer programs use a combination of a number of techniques, but it is not normally necessary for you to know these in detail.

BAR CHARTS AND GANTT CHARTS

Gantt charts, so called after the inventor Henry L Gantt, are a special form of bar chart.

The Gantt bar chart has horizontal columns. The details of the activities are written down the left-hand axis. These are usually in sequence with the first at the top. The timescale is then shown along the horizontal axis. These can be drawn on graph paper for accuracy.

The horizontal bars give the duration of the activity and are usually shown as blocks or lines, as shown in Figure 7.8. As tasks progress towards completion this can be shown by shading or a heavier line under the activity, as shown in Figure 7.9.

blocks

lines

FIGURE 7.8

50% complete

50% complete

FIGURE 7.9

One of the benefits of the Gantt chart is that it shows the sequence of activities for easy reference to help manage the project. It could also be used to represent specific requirements, such as manpower or resources. However, the decisions as to starting time and duration of each activity must come from an in-depth understanding of the potential complexities which could be encountered in the project.

Planning is easy if we consider examples where each activity starts at the beginning of the week and lasts for a finite number of weeks, as shown in Figure 7.10. The block refers to the timescale of the activity *not* the number of people/days estimated as required for completion. A real project would not necessarily fit in neatly like this and one would normally calculate timings to the day, rather than the week. For example, an activity could easily be scheduled to start on a Wednesday and last for an estimated nine working days. When estimating these working days, the manpower needs, or resources, are, of course, taken into consideration. So, looking at Figure 7.10, there could be only one person working on the digging for seven days (that is, 7 units) or two working for seven days (that is, 14 units); while only one person ordering for two days.

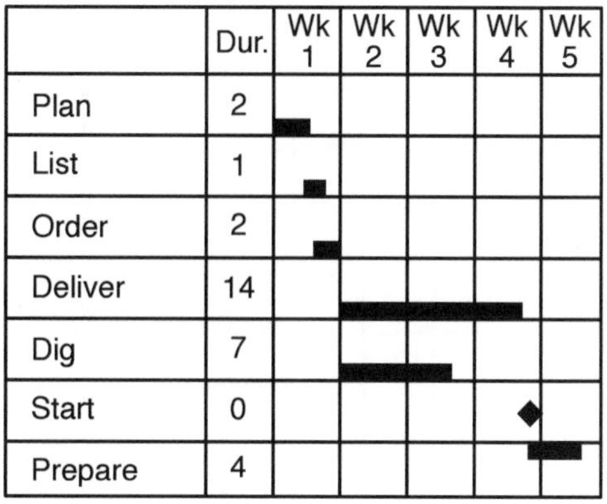

	Dur.	Wk 1	Wk 2	Wk 3	Wk 4	Wk 5
Plan	2	▪				
List	1	▪				
Order	2	▪				
Deliver	14		▬▬			
Dig	7		▬			
Start	0				◆	
Prepare	4					▬

FIGURE 7.10: Simple Gantt chart

No indication of these figures can be gleaned from the Gantt chart. However, separate manpower planning charts can be produced for cross reference, or the resources can be added to the Gantt chart. In most computerized charts the resources will be included in the one Gantt chart.

With Gantt bar charts, the milestone technique is easily achieved. As the name implies, a *milestone* point is:

A fixed point taken at any given time during the progress of a project where *actual* **progress can be compared directly against estimated progress.**

We can illustrate this on the simple example given in Figure 7.11. A milestone check has been set for the end of week five. This involves drawing a vertical line at this point on the time axis. We can then review this time point on each activity bar, comparing actual with expected progress.

Alternatively, milestones can be built into your chart as activities as we saw in Figure 7.6 with a duration of zero. At these points actual progress is checked against the planned milestone. In this method, milestones are usually critical events which must be achieved on the given date before further progress on the project is possible.

DEPENDENCIES

The simple Gantt chart we have looked at does not show which items are dependent on each other, although in the charts we have drawn the start dates for each activity have been shown by placing the bars in the correct position. Dependencies are essential for

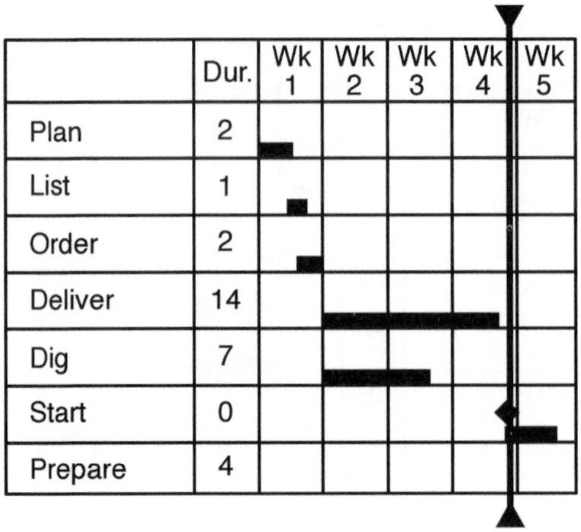

	Dur.	Wk 1	Wk 2	Wk 3	Wk 4	Wk 5
Plan	2					
List	1					
Order	2					
Deliver	14					
Dig	7					
Start	0					
Prepare	4					

FIGURE 7.11: Milestone on a Gantt chart

working out your critical path and finish dates and can easily be included by showing the links between activities and how each activity begins after its dependent activities have been completed. When your Gantt chart is complete, it will then show start and finish dates.

Computer programs which produce Gantt charts usually incorporate the facility to add dependencies and will then automatically show the critical path. We will look at this again in Chapter 14.

SESSION 7 – EXERCISES WITH YOUR TEAM

OVERVIEW

The following exercises will help your team to practise the stages required for making a simple project plan. There is also an idea for a further project planning exercise based on a 'real' project in your workplace.

In total these exercises could take 1–2 hours so you may prefer to divide this session into two. If so, we suggest you tackle Exercise 7.1 in one session, and Exercise 7.2 followed by the 'Further exercises' in another complete session.

EQUIPMENT AND MATERIALS

You will require a flip chart. The team will require sheets of paper or card (A6 size is ideal) and space to lay these out or pin them on a board.

Preparation and time notes are given separately for each exercise.

Exercise 7.1

Overview

This exercise will take the group through the process of producing a simple critical path chart using the example of making a pot of tea.

Equipment and materials

A flip chart, cards and pens.

Preparation

You will require copies of the answers (given at the end of the exercise) on a flip chart. Write these up before you begin. There are also 'Hints' to help the team. You can write these out on cards or the flip chart to give out when needed.

You may wish to write the instructions out and give them to your team as one or more handouts.

Method

This exercise can be carried out individually, in pairs, or as a whole group. We suggest a method of working initially in pairs, then bringing the group together for the final steps.

If the team consists of four or more, break into pairs.

Time

This exercise should take 40–50 minutes.

Steps

Step 1: Listing the activities

Ask the pairs to list the activities involved in making a cup of tea by the old method of making a pot of tea first. They should put the activities on their pieces of card (one activity per card).

Step 2: Adding resources

On each activity card ask them to add:

1. Resources (for example, one person, one kettle).
2. Lapsed time for that activity.

The result should look like Figure 7.12.

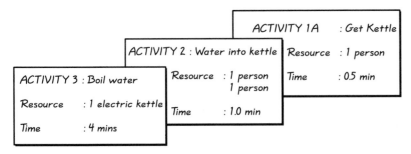

FIGURE 7.12

Step 3: Grouping and sequencing
Ask the pairs to sort out the sequence of their project. To do this for each activity they must decide:

1. What is the activity to do now?
2. What must be done before that can be done?
3. What can be done at the same time?
4. What must follow this activity?

Hint

The best way to do this is to sort the cards into the correct order on a large table or pinned to a board.

The result could look like Figure 7.13. You have worked out the sequence and dependencies in your plan.

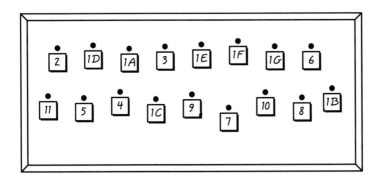

FIGURE 7.13

Step 4: Resourcing
If you have enough people to tackle all the activities which could be carried out simultaneously it could produce a plan like that shown in Figure 7.14.

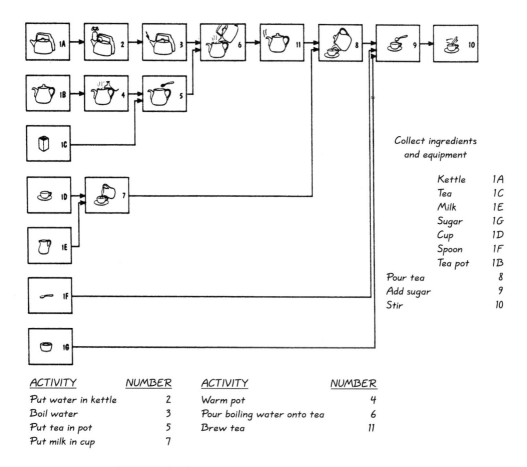

ACTIVITY	NUMBER	ACTIVITY	NUMBER
Put water in kettle	2	Warm pot	4
Boil water	3	Pour boiling water onto tea	6
Put tea in pot	5	Brew tea	11
Put milk in cup	7		

FIGURE 7.14

Discuss the results of Step 3 by considering how many of your pairs have made this assumption? How many have assumed only one person as the resource? You can now discuss how adding or taking away resources can affect the project plan.

Finally, as a group decide on a reasonable resource (for example, one or two people) and produce a consensus plan on this basis. Your plan will probably still look something like Figure 7.14.

Step 5: Latest start/earliest finish
Working in pairs, using the durations already written on the activity cards ask the pairs to work out the earliest start for each of the activities in their projects.

Hint

Give the following if it will help This is done by adding together the durations of all the activities from left to right across the diagram. Where two or more routes through the diagram meet, the earliest start is taken from the route which has taken the longest to complete.

When this has been done all the way through to activity 10, the finish date for the whole project can be calculated by adding the duration of the last activity to its earliest start time. The *latest finish* times are calculated by reversing the whole process, working from right to left. For instance, the latest finish time for activity 9 (Add sugar) is calculated by subtracting the duration of activity 10 (Stir) from the finish time for the whole project. Similarly, the latest finish time for activity 1G (Collect sugar) is calculated by subtracting the duration of activity 9 from the latest finish time for activity 9.

Step 6: Establishing the critical path
Ask the pairs to work out the critical path for the whole 'project'.

Hint

In this example activities on the critical path become obvious because they have no 'float', that is, their duration is exactly the same as the time available to do them. Any extra time required to do these activities will mean the project overruns its expected finish time.

Answer
In the tea making example, activities 1B, 1C, 1D, 1E, 1G 4, 5 and 7 each take 20 seconds (0.33 minutes). They are not 'critical' because 1B 4, 1C and 5 can be done well before 6 can start. 1D, 1E and 7 can be done well before 8 can start and 1F and 1G can be done before 9 starts. Even if one person does all these activities in sequence, they can all be done while activity 3 is in progress.

The answer, with times and the critical path, is shown in Figure 7.15.

CRITICAL PATH

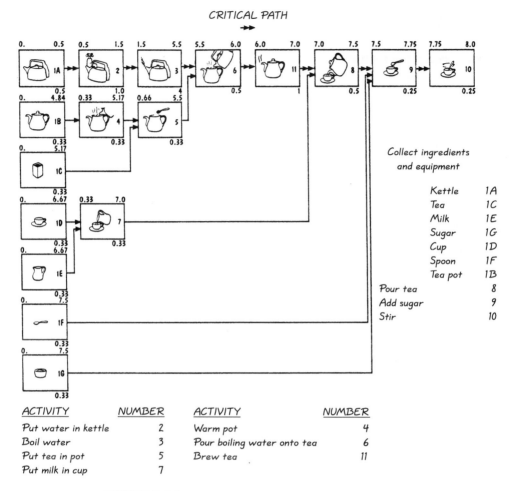

ACTIVITY	NUMBER	ACTIVITY	NUMBER
Put water in kettle	2	Warm pot	4
Boil water	3	Pour boiling water onto tea	6
Put tea in pot	5	Brew tea	11
Put milk in cup	7		

FIGURE 7.15

Conclusions

The 'resource management' conclusion reached from carrying out the critical path analysis is that the tea can still be ready in minimum total time even if only one person is used to make it.

FURTHER EXERCISES

We suggest that after the exercises above have been completed your team produces a plan for a 'real' project they may have to carry out; or you may now like to think about developing your own exercises to use with your team. The value of this is that you can use examples more closely related to real projects which your team may have to undertake in your own situation.

SUMMARY

BEGINNING TO PLAN

Project planning begins with deciding:

- Project objectives
- Project strategies.

A good plan specifies:

- policies
- tactics
- procedures
- objectives.

Good planners consider:

- What you are trying to achieve
- Why you are trying to achieve it
- When you are trying to achieve it by.

PRINCIPLES OF PLANNING

There are three key principles of planning:

1. Gather together all data available at the time.
2. Plans must be flexible working tools.
3. Choose the most appropriate technique.

To produce a good plan it is helpful to work through the stages to establish the activities, dependencies, time required and resources available.

DRAWING UP A PROJECT PLAN

Step 1   Sort project into chunks if complex. Describe every activity.

Step 2   Add information on resources and time.

Step 3   Sort into groups if complex. Sequence activities.

Step 4   Establish dependencies.

Step 5   Calculate earliest start and latest finish times.

Step 6   Establish the critical path. Review resourcing and dependencies if necessary.

BENEFITS AND WEAKNESSES OF NETWORKS

Networks have many benefits. As well as presenting inter-relationships among activities, they also represent the critical path for the schedule, aiding the monitoring and control of the project.

■ Networks are suitable for controlling complex projects and can be used with a computer, integrating with the Project Information System. However, there are several potential weaknesses of which the user should be aware:

– Networks do not permit manpower planning. As suggested earlier, a combination of both Gantt charts and networks should be considered to present this total spread of information.

– Although apparently giving precise, numerical constraints and deadlines, it must be remembered that your early figures are likely to be based on estimates – thus latest start times and floats should be treated with caution.

– Networks require a lot of skill to construct properly – care must be taken with both designing and using them, in case decisions are being made on incorrect assumptions.

CHAPTER 8

PRODUCING A PROJECT PLAN 2: RESOURCES

KEY LEARNING POINTS

- **Know how to use at least one technique for manpower planning**
- **Know how to allocate activities and responsibilities to resources**
- **Understand how to use resources most effectively to benefit the project**

RESOURCES

Up to this point we have looked at the background to project management and the benefits of using it. We have gone on to consider why and how good planning is the key to successful project management and looked at how to produce simple planning charts.

In order to plan really well and use these plans efficiently to monitor and control we really need more detailed information than we have considered so far. In Chapters 8 to 13 we will be going into this subject in more depth.

In Chapter 7 we looked at a variety of techniques for planning the project schedules. So far, though, we have not looked in detail at the effect of resources on this. No single technique will give a total picture of project resource requirements, but by combining resource allocation and manpower planning with time schedules, a picture can be built up. Although resources can include equipment and materials as well as other items, in this chapter we will concentrate on manpower as this is the most important resource. It is also sometimes the most difficult to control!

MANPOWER PLANNING

Planning your manpower will help to smooth the requirements for any project and will help to identify potential troublespots. With reference to overall manpower availability, it will also allow the flexibility to transfer manpower to respond to peaks and troughs – as well as the occasional crisis!

The Gantt bar charts and networks which we have been considering so far give us a detailed indication of how a project will progress. In order to design these, we have had to make estimates with regard to how long each activity will take to be completed. These estimates, in turn, will have presupposed certain manpower levels and availability of resources. These details are not included on the networks we have seen so far, so they must be represented somehow. In computer generated charts these are automatically combined, as we will see in Chapter 14; but to understand fully resource and manpower planning you should first understand the techniques for creating these manually.

Manpower planning charts, of 'manpower against time', can be drawn for:

- A particular skill or trade
- Groups of particular skills or trades
- An individual activity
- Activities packages
- The overall project.

You may not require all of these; exactly what you need will, to some extent, depend on the complexity of the overall project. The simplest way to begin planning is to establish the manpower requirements for each activity. From this most of the other charts or requirements can be developed. You can also use it to help you accommodate changes.

Because of the inter-relationships of manpower requirements

on virtually all aspects of projects, fluctuations on one activity can have a knock-on effect on subsequent activities. For example, referring back to our wall building example in Chapter 7, delays in completing the delivery of materials would mean that the bricklaying team would be idle until this was completed. Unless this initial time-slip is made up, the whole project could progressively slip behind schedule. In its simplest form this could be shown as a graph of work as shown in Figure 8.1.

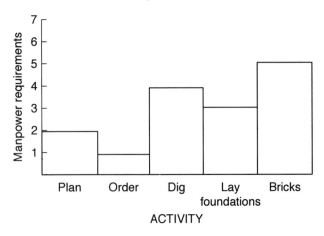

FIGURE 8.1: Manpower by activity

This is of limited use, but it is a starting point; for by planning our needs by allocating resources to the tasks, we can establish how long this work will take as shown in Figure 8.2. This then shows us that we could complete Task 1 in 1 day, and Task 5 in 2 days. If we

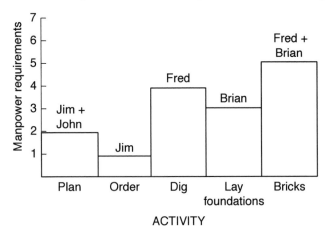

FIGURE 8.2: Manpower by activity with resource allocation

Task	Dur.	Res.	Day 1	2	3	4	5	6	7	8	9	10	11	12
Plan	1	Ji + Jo	▄											
Order	1	Ji		▄										
Dig	4	Fr				▄▄▄▄								
Lay foundations	3	Br								▄▄▄				
Bricks	2½	Fr + Br											▄▄▄	

FIGURE 8.3: Gantt Chart showing activities, resource allocation and timing

transferred this to a timing plan, it could give us the simple Gantt chart shown in Figure 8.3.

SKILLS

We cannot, however, arbitrarily allocate the tasks to people without taking account of what they can do, that is, what their skills are.

The simple Gantt chart shown in Figure 8.3 combined skills and time planning because in Figure 8.2 we had allocated resources with specific skills to the individual activities. As we have seen earlier in the wall building example, particular skills can relate directly to activities, either singly or by identifying particular skills required during any given activity or activity package.

If we are working on more complex projects, with many resources and a large number of skill requirements, we may need to do more detailed skills planning. Subdividing total manpower planning requirements into individual skills requirements is obviously a necessary step to allow internal scheduling of skills and trades for a complex project. It will also highlight where external resources may be required to enable schedules to be met.

RESPONSIBILITIES

As well as general manpower allocation to specific activities and activity packages, it is important to establish and record responsibilities. This helps both the project leader and the individuals concerned to monitor responsibility and progress. The responsibilities are set out on a matrix, as shown in Figure 8.4.

As well as general manpower allocation it is important to establish and record responsibilities

	E	W	O	D
Planning	S			P
Ordering	P	S		
Bricklaying		P		
Digging		P		
Material supply			P	
Inspection	P			

Key

Dept. responsible   Responsibility

E = Engineering   P = Primary
W = Contract workers   S = Secondary
O = Offsite supplier
D = Drawing office

FIGURE 8.4: Responsibilities matrix

This matrix gives both clear, identifiable responsibilities and accountability at the lowest level required. The activities areas are taken from the appropriate Gantt chart of activities sequence, or the activities from a network. More detail could be added by including names of actual team members.

RESOURCE PLANNING IN PRACTICE

Consider this situation in the wall building project:

The planned time for 'dig foundations' is four days. On day two it rains heavily and the trench becomes waterlogged. Work is abandoned and overnight the sides slip into the trench.

This part of the project is delayed by two days. Brian has another job lined up to begin on day 15 (when he was due to complete the bricklaying).

What would you do? If you have another member of the team available to help out with the appropriate skills you might get the job done on time or even earlier; or you might have to bring in someone extra. How would the rest of the team react to that?

As we have indicated in the example above, manpower planning must go deeper than merely ensuring that the correct number of bodies is in the right place, at the right time. It is dangerously easy in project management to forget that the figures in a table or the blocks on a graph represent human beings. If working too close to the planning process, one can often underestimate the effects of personnel inter-relationships during a project.

For example, consider this project:

The project is for the installation of robotics in a factory production line. The project leader has carried out her research and produced her networks and manpower plans, calling for 20 robotics installation engineers to work on converting the line. What might the effect be on the:

■ Factory supervisors, required to cope with this sudden influx of engineers?
■ Morale of the workforce and resultant change in productivity?
■ General working atmosphere, reflecting on the project team morale and productivity?
■ Project leader's credibility, both with her own team and the general workforce?
■ Attitudes towards the introduction of robotics, regardless of prior discussions, caused by the sheer size and suddenness of the operation?
■ Long-term benefits of the transfer to robotics use in the factory?

These implications would have to be considered closely at the early project and manpower planning stages. You would need not only to plan the requirements of the job, but the knock-on effects of what you will be doing. You might ask the following questions:

■ Whose job is it?
■ Need you consult someone else? Who?
■ Do you need meetings and training to explain what you are doing and why?

The answers to these could result in further negotiations and delays. So it is always important to consider *all* aspects and effects of your project as early as possible in the planning process. It is no good ignoring problems and hoping they will go away; they must be addressed and solutions found. It is well to remember that an effective *two-way* communication process is necessary to keep any project progressing positively. Over and above this, informal communication can often identify and establish solutions for potential problems at an early stage of their development.

An effective two-way communication process is necessary to keep any project progressing positively

SESSION 8 – EXERCISE WITH YOUR TEAM

OVERVIEW

This exercise will help you to add resource planning to the techniques you learned in Chapter 7.

For this exercise you will need to refer back to the exercises you carried out at the end of Chapter 7. If you completed the further exercises the project chosen for that would be the best one to use here.

EQUIPMENT AND MATERIALS

You will require a flip chart and the team will need paper and pens.

PREPARATION

You will need to prepare Step 1 below (draw up a chart with columns) in advance. You will also require the project plan you prepared for the last exercise.

METHOD

Most of this exercise should be carried out by discussion with the team.

TIME

This exercise will take approximately 20–30 minutes.

Exercise 8.1

Steps

Look at the example project plan you produced for the last exercise in Chapter 7.

1. Draw up a chart with columns. List all the activities in the left-hand column and the expected duration in the next column. Appoint someone to act as scribe or do it yourself.
2. Now with your team, brainstorm and for each activity list the resources with the available skills.
3. Now, by discussions assuming all resources could be used, work out the minimum time for each activity.
4. By how much does this shorten your project?
5. Finally, discuss with your team whether this is feasible and sensible (that is, even if two people are qualified, could they really share an activity and halve the time?). Then revise your plan into a realistic resource allocation.

SUMMARY

Although resources may include a variety of items such as equipment, the most important resource in a project is normally manpower.

Manpower planning charts can be produced to show manpower against time for:

■ A particular skill or trade
■ Groups of skills or trades
■ Individual activities
■ Activities packages
■ The overall project.

Manpower requirements are inter-related with all activities in the project and fluctuations in one activity can have knock-on effects on all subsequent activities.

Resource planning should not be in isolation or without consideration for the human elements. Personnel inter-relationships can have important implications for the success of a project. They may mean that the project manager should discuss some aspects of the project with individuals beyond the project team.

Early planning, addressing likely problems up front and two-way communication are important activities in resource planning and management.

CHAPTER 9

PRODUCING A PROJECT PLAN 3: CONSIDERING THE BUDGET

KEY LEARNING POINTS

- Know how to produce a budget
- Produce a budget which is as accurate as possible
- Understand potential problems with budgeting and how to overcome them
- Know the reasons for budget overruns and how to avoid them
- Know how to construct a time-phased budget

WAYS OF PLANNING THE BUDGET

In most management roles you will be expected to produce budgets. These can cover anything from the purchase of small one-

Most of the basic principles of budgeting apply to planning the budget for a project

off items to the total ongoing cost of running a complete factory. Most of the basic principles of budgeting apply to planning the budget for a project. The main differences are in linking it to time and resources. We will illustrate this by going back to our simple example, building a wall.

> You would start by listing all the items you would need to purchase and services you will have to buy. You would then get estimates or quotes for these items and add it all up. This is the amount you would need to spend to get what you want, that is, your *budget* for the job.
>
> The next question is, 'When will you have to pay for this?' Some items may require a deposit up-front, others can be paid on a 30-day invoice. By putting this into your plan, you can produce a simple cash flow forecast. For example, the brick company may require a deposit on receipt of order in March, deliver for fitting in April and invoice in April for May payment. the bricklayer has no cash outlay so does not ask for a deposit but wants payment immediately for his work in April.

Your budget could look something like that shown in Table 9.1.

TABLE 9.1: Cash flow plan for wall building

ITEM	TOTAL COST	MARCH	APRIL	MAY
Bricks	750	75		675
Bricklaying	560		560	
Mortar	150	15		145
Dig foundations	320		320	
Capping stones	160	16		144
Totals	1940	106	880	964

This shows a small expenditure at the outset and major items in each of the next two months.

This is a relatively straightforward project on which you can obtain accurate quotes and plan payment with the activities over a relatively short time. A more complex project, with many more activities over a longer period, would be more complicated but the basic principles are the same. However, there is one aspect that this simple plan does not cover and that is the question of contingencies. Contingencies enable us to plan for the unexpected, to put money into the project in case it is needed for unexpected situations. We will look at this in more detail later in this chapter.

Budgets and deadlines are the most obvious indicators of the progress of a project. Also, the final business evaluation of a project is invariably based on cost. So, before we go on to consider how you should plan your budget, we will look at some of the potential pitfalls and how to avoid them.

GETTING IT RIGHT

Overruns in time and cost are normally seen as a failure in project management. In extreme circumstances they could be a disaster. The crash of giants such as Lockheed and Rolls Royce in 1971 resulted from the cost overrun on a single project. The Sydney Opera House was estimated to cost $A 6 million in 1967. On final completion in 1973, the total cost was $A 100 million. Twenty per cent of North Sea oil fields were up to 200 per cent cost overrun.

Many more examples can be found if we care to look – but do we use these to learn from? Too often we do not. It is much easier to file away disasters and forget them. What project managers must do is analyse them and learn from them. Whenever something does not go as expected, we must turn it into a learning experience and ask:

- What happened?
- Why did it happen?
- How can I prevent it happening again?

Then turn that knowledge into a resource for future planning.

> Overruns in time and cost are normally seen as a failure in project management. In extreme circumstances they could be a disaster

GOING INTO THE UNKNOWN

The earliest stages of cost planning are the key to getting your project budgets right. In Chapter 2 we looked at the Concorde project and saw that it overran in both cost and time. This was largely due to the fact that it was a 'development' project so it involved many unknown factors. Even when a project is not going into the unknown in the way Concorde was, there are likely to be some costs which are difficult to quote accurately. In such cases, you must gather together *all* the available evidence. This should include lessons learned from past experience, as well as information directly related to this project. We said earlier in this chapter that there is a

> The earliest stages of cost planning are the key to getting your project budgets right

tendency to ignore failures, but in gathering information for every new project the lessons learned from failures as well as successes should be taken into account.

WHY ARE BUDGETS INACCURATE?

If you consider the reasons why budgets are so frequently inaccurate you may be able to avoid some of these mistakes yourself. Firstly, most estimates are made by the very people who want to undertake the project. This means they are likely to produce a 'favourable' budget to ensure that the project gets approval. They may either be working on the assumption that once the project is well under way, additional funds will be found rather than having to abandon it. Or they could just be looking at it with rose-coloured spectacles and genuinely believe they can meet this cost – although they have blocked out of their mind potential problems.

Secondly, costs for projects are supposed to be based on facts, but the only real *fact* that is ever established is the final cost. The physicist, Einstein, once said, 'Cost is supposed to be based on facts, but the facts are wrong!'

Thirdly, project costs are spread over a period of time and the cost for an activity in 1996 is unlikely to be the same as in 1997 or 1998. Costs are too often planned without taking account of time – this is very risky. Even if you can agree fixed prices with some suppliers, they will be unable to hold them indefinitely. Time overruns almost always mean cost overruns, and even if time is on target, projects with long time spans are subject to many unpredictable elements.

> 'Cost is supposed to be based on facts, but the facts are wrong!'

THE MAIN CAUSES

The main ingredients which cause cost overruns can be summarized as:

1. Optimistic budgets based on limited technical definition
2. Excessive delays – either in approval or project duration
3. Unscheduled scope changes or hazards
4. Spiralling inflation
5. Unexpected fluctuations in currency
6. Project mismanagement.

OVERCOMING THE COST TRAPS

BUDGET ESTIMATES TOO LOW

This is a situation experienced frequently given the usual constraints of a project, especially a long-term one. Despite allowances for inflation and attempts to foresee every eventuality, low estimates can soon be exceeded if not monitored carefully. This can lead to several problems.

CASH FLOW CRISES

Where estimates have been too low for any given phase, the project could run into cash flow problems. This could affect phased payments to contractors and similar actions, with a knock-on effect on their cash flows as well.

NEGATIVE PROFIT PROJECT

Low estimates on the final costs of a project can create a 'negative profit' situation, where the company is locked into a project which has exceeded estimates to such an extent that it cannot be profitable.

A number of the examples of project failures we have described show how, once started, the organization was committed to the project, although it exceeded time and cost estimates to such a large extent that it would never be profitable.

FIXED PRICE CONTRACTS

Where a contractor is on a fixed price contract and costs have greatly exceeded estimates without changes to the contract specifications, there is a danger that the contractor could go bankrupt. Project leaders must monitor this situation closely as there will be situations where the failure of a contractor supplying specialist components or services to a project could jeopardize the whole project. Where this could arise, it may well be in the project's interest to review the value of the contract – although this must be done carefully and objectively against clearly written specifications.

BUDGET ESTIMATES TOO HIGH

Although less likely to happen in a commercially viable project with open tenders, this situation can arise in new development projects. In this event, where the client and/or contractors could be involved in totally new techniques or technologies, high estimates can be caused by allowing too high contingency percentages. Although apparently not such a financial problem as where estimates are too low, the situation can create problems.

CREATES A '*LAISSEZ-FAIRE*' ATTITUDE

Where there is an unrealistic, 'easy' estimate, this can affect team motivation and performance. The lack of financial pressures can lead to poor control of the project, potentially allowing costs to escalate even beyond the easy estimates. A similar atmosphere can be created where contractors believe that project and contractual changes will lead to revised and/or additional budgets. Where initial estimates were over–generous, new cost targets should be set and these should be worked to with the same requirements as before, that is, they must not be exceeded.

UNECONOMICAL USE OF FUNDS AND RESOURCES

Where too high estimates are accepted by the client, this obviously places an unnecessary drain on total resources. In simple terms, a small project for a department which is approved at, say, £4000 may seem of minor importance where the company overall has budgeted for a £150 000 spend on such projects in the financial year. However, when this £150 000 is apportioned to departments, your particular department may only be allowed a total of around £9000 for small projects for the year. Committing almost half the budget to one project then takes on a new significance.

From the contractor's point of view, a project with a high profit margin can be used as a justification for high capital expenditure. This can have benefits, but, equally, can get out of hand if not controlled. This may result in initial profits, in real terms, slipping away.

POTENTIAL HIGH RISK AREAS

Look out for areas of the project which could lead to:

- Inaccurate estimating
- Small changes to design
- Small omissions – subsequently added but considered as part of the original estimate
- Small extras – are they costed in the project proposal?
- Unforeseen problems requiring corrective actions
- Variations inherent in the estimating methods.

Insist on clear guidelines for good practice in project specification

Insist on clear guidelines for good practice in project specification. To some extent, awareness of these potential traps can only come from experience. Any lack of experience, however, can be augmented by:

- Checking back on objective reports/records of previous, similar projects to establish potential problem areas.

- Discussing the project and potential pitfalls with others with more experience of project management.
- Objective consideration of parts of the project which have 'unknown areas' which might become a direct cost liability.
- Carrying out further feasibility and development work prior to launching the project to remove areas of technical uncertainty.
- Awareness of possible areas which traditionally have 'unknowns' and expecting the worst from them. This helps to estimate contingency amounts necessary. Some examples of this might be:
  - Weather and soil consistency conditions in building projects.
  - New component development/production costs.
  - Delays caused by 'committee management' on large-scale projects.

So, what other steps can you take to avoid these traps?

1. Do not be over-optimistic. Always take the time to make a detailed assessment of project costs before you start.
2. Link costs to time and build in contingencies for inflation and other time-related factors.
3. Consider resource requirements and any extra costs if different or additional resources are required.
4. Gather *all* the evidence available (talk to colleagues, learn from their experiences as well as your own).
5. Ask yourself to what extent this is a 'development' project and if so does it require contingencies for unknowns in terms of cost and time.
6. Ensure the project is properly monitored and controlled (we will deal with this in Chapters 10 to 13).

ESTIMATING FOR INFLATION

It is virtually impossible to predict inflation over, say, the life of a five-year project. Using computer models we can project current trends into the future, but this is not, strictly speaking, inflation forecasting. Traditionally, two methods have been applied:

1. Adding on a nominal percentage figure.
2. (In manufacturing industries and retail) inflating the new product price proportionately.

The first method is too simplistic, especially for a long-term project. The second has been nullified by market competition and recent government legislation. We are, therefore, left with the conclusion that prevention (or avoidance) is better than cure (or remedial action). What strategies can help this prevention?

Prevention is better than cure

SOME STRATEGIES FOR ESTIMATING FOR INFLATION

SHORT-TERM RENEWAL CONTRACTS
Contracts or projects lasting several years should be made on shorter-term renewal bases to allow for periodic renegotiations in line with inflation. Alternatively, contracts should incorporate appropriate escalation clauses which would be index-linked.

ALLOWANCE FOR CONTRACTUAL CONSTRAINTS
Some contracts providing progress payments (past MOD contracts are good examples) often exclude certain categories of cost and do not allow for subsequent flexibility. Where future inflexibility is built into the contract by the client, this must be taken into account (in terms of contingency amounts) when estimating contract costs.

STATING COSTS WITH INDICES
This is only necessary in projects which will spread over a long period (at least one year). When estimating long-term costs, today's figures should be stated with indices forward from this date. Predictions of costs to completion and at completion using different indices can be worked out to give useful estimates. The only practical way of demonstrating these effects is to produce simulation models, probably using computer models.

ESTIMATING CONTINGENCY ALLOWANCES

Within any project, some potential activities or activity packages will be less well-defined than others at an early stage of estimating. Thus, it is not accurate enough to add a flat percentage contingency amount for every section or phase of the project – each section must be considered separately and a contingency amount set relative to any areas of uncertainty expected.

It is not accurate enough to add a flat percentage contingency amount for every section or phase of the project

This can be added as a percentage to the basic estimated cost for that particular activity package. For example, this could be at least 25 per cent in the case of a research and development project because of the probability of changes in design and scope of the project.

It can be useful and effective to have a contingency bank account – a flexible budget amount to deal quickly and effectively with identified solutions. However, use of this account must be controlled carefully – it is to be used to meet *small* contingencies which otherwise might delay or upset the project, not as a fund to cover up for poor project management.

Major changes to the design or specification of the project will require new estimates – probably with separate, additional costing centres. They will certainly have to be dealt with through the formal change control system, as extra to the initial contract and estimates.

TIME-PHASED BUDGETS

As we have shown above, cost planning is linked directly with resources planning and work activity; so the cost planning is only one part of the total picture. The budget needs to be *time-phased* so that the costs are related to the various activities and associated resource requirements throughout the life of the project. We looked at this in a simple form in Table 9.1, but this only related to the cash flow for a very short-term project and did not require any contingency budgets.

> Costs must be related to the various activities and associated resource requirements throughout the life of the project

The graph shown in Figure 6.1 in Chapter 6 shows that the proposal phase incurs the lowest costs, yet has the biggest potential impact on overall costs. At this initial stage, costs would largely be estimates based on:

1. Previous experience
2. Best available advice
3. Supplier quotations (based on your best guess at the specification)
4. An inflation figure (estimated) to cover the estimated project duration.

To give more realistic estimates of cost, work, resource and manpower plans should be developed at the detailed activity level. However, in development or innovative projects it might be very difficult to give an objective estimate to some activities even then.

ACTIVITY PACKAGES

To make budgeting and controlling the project easier, each cost should be allocated to an activity. In large projects, it is sensible to devise a coding system which is compatible with your company's accounting system.

Each activity package should have a unique code number. This code is usually the lowest level to which costs will be applied. The accountability for budget will, therefore, also be allocated to each activity package – in other words, every activity which takes place during the project will have costs as well as time and resources allocated to it. The detail for these costs will come from:

- The cost estimates for the activity
- The work plan
- The manpower plan.

Details in the project plan regarding float time and earliest start/latest finish times will allow us to establish the reporting periods for the project and the priority areas because of their criticality. By adding the costs to the activity plan we can tie these in to the reporting periods and establish the most critical areas for monitoring and control. At the end of each reporting period the costs will be monitored – as well as time and other project controls. However, this does not mean that every cost should not be controlled as it is incurred. Checking costs against budget every time a new cost is incurred is an excellent way of controlling costs.

Manpower plans will also help us to see the budget requirements which relate to direct labour costs, bought in labour costs to meet peak demands or specific expertise requirements plus any other resource implications.

MAKING TIME-PHASED BUDGETS

Details for the time-phased budget will be based on:

1. Activity cost estimates (cost for each activity or activity package)
2. Work plan (timing of costs)
3. Manpower plan (cost for wages and other labour costs).

This information is then brought together within the time-phased budget. Cost estimates for each given activity can be subdivided into relative proportions for each reporting period (weekly, monthly, quarterly or whatever).

The amount of expenditure for each reporting period will be worked out to reflect the expenditure on resources, purchases and so on expected for that period. By adding up all these amounts for each period, it will give us the time-phased budget like the one shown in Table 9.2.

TABLE 9.2: Time-phased budget

ACTIVITY NAME/ LABEL	TOTAL ACTIVITY COST EST.	REPORTING PERIODS (MONTHLY) PHASED BUDGET							
		1	2	3	4	5	6	7	8
A	6500	5000		1500					
B	9000		3000		3000		3000		
C	5000			1000	1000	1000	1000	1000	
D	5000				1000	1000	1000	1000	1000
E	7000			2000	2000		2000	1000	
F	3000			500	500	500	500	500	500
G	2500							2500	
H	6000					2000			4000
Totals		5000	3000	5000	7500	4500	7500	6000	5500

As you can see, it is not all that different from the simple example shown in Table 9.1. If required, this time-phased budget can be balanced against money coming into the project to produce a cash flow forecast.

CHANGING BUDGETS

As we have already said, it is important that you gather as much information as possible to get the budget as accurate as you can, as early as possible. But there may be situations where budgets have to be altered.

Project plans may have to change due to unforeseen situations. However well the project has been planned, there is some element of subjective judgement which may be proved wrong in reality. So your plans must be flexible enough to take account of *legitimate* alterations. However, budgets should *not* be changes because:

Plans must be flexible enough to take account of legitimate alterations, but not bad planning or lack of control

- Progress is too slow
- The project is working inefficiently
- Initial estimates were poor
- Prices were inaccurately quoted.

Budgets should only be changed if there is no other route. But most of these points should be accurately estimated from the outset. To be a good control tool, the budget must be accurate.

SESSION – EXERCISES WITH YOUR TEAM

OVERVIEW

These exercises are intended to help your team plan a project budget. They build on exercises and information in earlier sessions. The outcome of Exercise 9.1 could be used to produce your own checklist as a job aid.

EQUIPMENT AND MATERIALS

You will require a flip chart and pen.

PREPARATION

You should prepare the flip chart for Exercise 9.1 by writing each of the three questions on one sheet. You will also need to refer back to the list of reasons given in the sections of this chapter entitled 'Why are budgets inaccurate?' and 'Overcoming the cost traps' and also the summary of this chapter. You may wish to write down the key points as notes to use in your learning session.

For Exercise 9.2, prepare a pro forma time-phased budget using Table 9.2 to help. You may also wish to write up the 'Hint' to give to your team for guidance.

METHOD

These exercises are carried out by brainstorming and discussion.

TIME

Exercise 9.1 will take approximately 20–30 minutes. Exercise 9.2 will take approximately 30–40 minutes.

Exercise 9.1

Steps

1. With your team, brainstorm on the following questions:
   - What are the main tools for defining project budgets?
   - What are the main problems with making accurate budgets?
   - What measures can you take to overcome these problems?
2. When you have brainstormed and discussed these you can look back at the sections on budget inaccuracies and cost

traps and the summary of this chapter and add any ideas which have not been covered.

3. You might find it useful to collect the results of this discussion in a simple list and ask one or more of the team to produce a job aid which you could use as an *aide-mémoire* next time you have to cost a project.

Exercise 9.2

Steps

1. We suggest the team select a project as a group then initially work in pairs on producing their plans. After 10–15 minutes this should be shared and one plan drawn on the flip chart. If you do not have a suitable example of your own, use the following:

    You are planning the installation of a new computer network. Decide how many areas it will cover and how many different software packages it will include (new and specially written).

2. Using the example given in Table 9.2, draw up a time-phased budget for any project with which you are familiar. This could be one you have undertaken in the past or one you are currently working on or planning.

Hint

You will need to begin by listing all the activities required, with timescales, then divide these up into reporting periods. For every activity you will need to estimate the resources and any other expenditure and therefore the costs.

If this is a 'real project' you may be able to call on activity and resources plans already in place. If not, use your judgement to make realistic estimates for the purpose of this exercise.

SUMMARY

Simple budgets can be planned as cash flow forecasts to show income and outgoings in the project.

Past experience is a valuable resource for future planning – use your own and the experience of others to help accurate budgeting. Consider why others have made mistakes to help you avoid mistakes yourself. When estimating project costs you must consider *all* possible areas of expenditure.

The main causes of cost overrun are:

- Over–optimistic budgets
- Excessive project delays
- Unscheduled changes or hazards
- Spiralling inflation
- Unexpected currency fluctuations
- Project mismanagement.

Cost traps can be avoided by:

- Avoiding budget estimates which are too low or too high
- Not being too optimistic
- Planning for inflation and contingencies
- Linking costs to time
- Linking costs to resources
- Gathering *all* the available evidence
- Allowing contingencies for the unknown in 'development' projects
- Monitoring and controlling the project properly.

Time-phased budgets will give an accurate plan of cost expenditure during the life of the project and allow more effective monitoring and control.

Changes to budgets should be avoided unless there are *legitimate* reasons and budgets should be flexible enough to allow for necessary changes.

To be a good control tool, the budget must be accurate.

CHAPTER 10

MONITORING AND CONTROL

KEY LEARNING POINTS

- Know the difference between monitoring and control
- Understand the benefits of control
- Know how to use plans to aid control
- Know how to deal with project changes and the benefits of change control
- Know how to analyse the performance of the project

WHY MONITOR?

Quite simply you need to monitor the progress of your project to see what is happening, whether it is on course or if it needs any corrective action.

Let us illustrate this by a simple example:

> If you were driving a car blindfolded but knew where you wanted to get to, you would set off on a course in the direction which you believed would take you to your planned destination. You would probably carry on along this course until you hit something or fell off the edge of the road. Then you would have to do something to rectify the situation. You might even find your car irreparably damaged.

This sounds like a pretty stupid example – you would never allow someone to drive a car blindfolded. That is, however, exactly what you are doing if you set off on a project but are not constantly monitoring your progress – which is exactly what a driver normally does during the course of a journey. As you drive along you look ahead and adjust your speed and direction accordingly. You do not wait until you hit something before you take avoiding action. We have already stressed the importance of planning. If you have carried this out correctly, you will know where you are trying to get to during the course of the project and you will know the parameters within which you must work. Then you should be constantly checking progress and looking ahead to see where you are now and where the present course is taking you.

The monitoring process is even more important in projects where the planning has involved a high degree of 'guesstimation' – such as research projects. Because the planning stage may only be based on partial facts as the project progresses, this information should become more accurate and enable you to revise and develop your plans more and more accurately.

> The monitoring process is even more important in projects where the planning has involved a high degree of 'guesstimation' – such as research projects

WHY CONTROL?

There is no point in monitoring your progress unless you use that information to keep you on course. When you check your progress you then make any necessary adjustments on the way. This is the control process.

Project plans may require change during the lifetime of the project, as we have already said, especially where the original plans were based on incomplete information. You might even have to consider a proceed/abort decision if things are going badly wrong; the earlier this is done the more cost effective it will be. So it is essential to monitor regularly the project from its earliest stages and implement control procedures all along the way.

PLANNING TO AID CONTROL

We have already looked at the planning process at some length and considered how important it is. But to use the project plans to control your project you need to be sure you have considered all the available facts and especially the high risk areas.

THE PROJECT CONTROL CYCLE

The cycle is shown in Figure 10.1. In any cyclical control process, reference is being made:

- *Backwards at each stage*   To compare actual with projected progress and to review and potentially revise targets.
- *Forwards at each stage*   To establish extra activities required to attain existing targets.

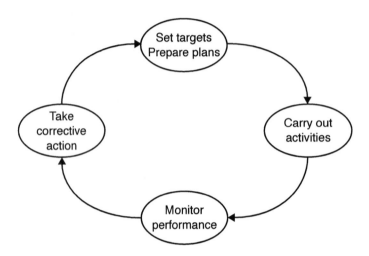

FIGURE 10.1: The project control cycle

The inter-relationship of the stages need not, therefore, be strictly as represented in the cycle. In fact, it is more like a series of spirals than one circle! The importance is rather in the continuous inter-relation of the actions. One must also consider the cycle as continuing, as each rotation reaches a more detailed level of the overall plan.

Using the cyclical approach, the project leader and team can monitor progress, compensate or push where necessary to maintain progress and incorporate and control change (where it has been established as necessary).

AIDS TO CONTROL

There are a number of items which have an important role in helping to maintain control during the project, at handover and after commissioning. These include:

- Operating manuals
- Control manuals
- Diagnostic charts to support subsequent operations

- A training plan
- Definition of regular post-commissioning audit procedures to maintain performance
- Checking of each aspect of the project against specifications for performance before handover
- Contractual arrangements with suppliers of equipment
- Provision of diagnostic aids and material to support training.

These items are only of value if they are used in all areas of the project because control needs to take place in all areas. Monitoring and control of these different areas, covering the types of considerations listed in Figure 10.2, will be achieved through a combination of reports, site visits and an effective reporting structure and progress for related meetings. These are summarized in Figure 10.2 and the relationship to the project control cycle is shown.

With reference to the data generated by these activities, the project manager will be in a position to exercise control over any slippage through actions such as alterations to the organizational structures (administration procedures, reporting relationships and so on); pressure on suppliers and sub-contractors; technical audits on design stages and progress and financial reviews.

WHAT PROBLEMS CAN HAPPEN?

Projects can go off course in a number of ways and these can easily be grouped under the three headings of the project management triangle. There are also tell-tale signs which you should look out for to alert you to potential problems.

QUALITY PROBLEMS

These can be seen by:

- Too many 'head banging' meetings with sub-contractors or suppliers
- Too many things having to be rejected and done again.

COST PROBLEMS

These can be seen by:

- Too much overtime being worked by project team members and suppliers
- Cash flow falling behind predictions
- Too many invoices coming in over budget.

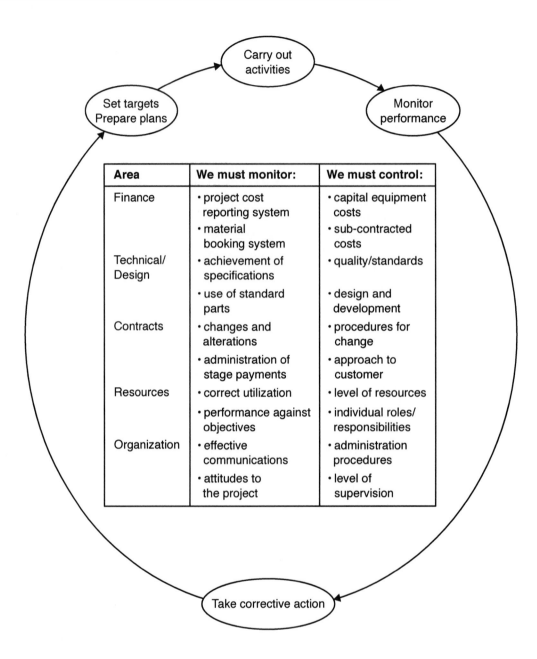

Area	We must monitor:	We must control:
Finance	• project cost reporting system	• capital equipment costs
	• material booking system	• sub-contracted costs
Technical/ Design	• achievement of specifications	• quality/standards
	• use of standard parts	• design and development
Contracts	• changes and alterations	• procedures for change
	• administration of stage payments	• approach to customer
Resources	• correct utilization	• level of resources
	• performance against objectives	• individual roles/ responsibilities
Organization	• effective communications	• administration procedures
	• attitudes to the project	• level of supervision

FIGURE 10.2: Monitoring and control procedures

TIME PROBLEMS

These can be seen by:

- Too many 'almost complete tasks'
- Too many 'priority actions' listed
- Milestones not being achieved

- Large numbers of panic meetings
- Additional resources being drafted in to assist in critical areas.

When you look at the lists above they are pretty obvious – but there is no point in noting these effects without doing something about them. It is what you do when you see the signs which will save your project.

WHY DOES IT HAPPEN?

The next, and most important, step is for your to find out the reasons why these things are going wrong. The main reasons for cost escalation and late completion are:

- Poor leadership and poor integration of the team
- Technical complexity
- Poor project structure
- Poor organization
- Poor accountability
- A badly integrated information system
- Lack of focus and poor communications
- Unclear or inaccurate specifications

You will see from this list that the keys to getting the project working well are:

- A clear, full and accurate project plan
- Good communications between all involved
- Good management and teamwork.

None of these are very difficult and all are important skills which any successful manager will acquire and use.

COMMUNICATIONS

In Chapter 8 we have already mentioned the importance of formal two-way communications to keep the project progressing positively. Over and above this, information communication can often identify and establish solutions for trends at an early stage of their development. Every company/department has its 'grapevine' and, if the atmosphere and motivation are positive and active in the project team as well as between them and the 'user' environment, many potential problems can be solved before reaching the stage of requiring formal action.

At the more formal level, especially with the larger-scale project, communication channels (for example, formal reporting) can bring this information together, given positive control and leadership. Positive action relies on experienced supervisors, managers and project leaders.

On occasion, suitably motivated individuals at activity level can see the wider implications of a trend in that activity, if they are aware of the broader activity package. The middle course must be found, giving a combination of both controlled informal communication (following 'ground rules') and the formal project control hierarchy, thus establishing progress against targets and performance criteria.

In project communication a balance must be found between controlled informal communication and formal project control hierarchy

CONTROL BASELINES

A good project management system will integrate its planning systems and derive control baselines from detailed time-phased plans. This is done by taking the overall project plan, deriving work plans and cost estimates from this, then breaking these down into more detail to provide a template to work to – this is your *control baseline*. This is shown in Figure 10.3.

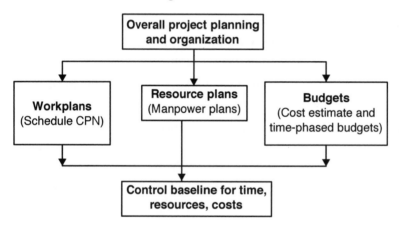

FIGURE 10.3: Deriving control baselines

Most computer generated project plans will allow you to set this baseline and keep it in the plan, so that as you make changes and update your plan the baseline remains for you to compare. We will look at using computers in Chapter 14.

FEATURES OF A PROJECT CONTROL SYSTEM

A good project control system:

1. Evaluates performance/progress objectively.
2. Structures plans and feedback to provide detailed analysis as required.

3. Applies a combination of formal and informal information, in a controlled way.
4. Identifies trends early enough to take corrective action.
5. Forecasts final completion costs and timescales, using performance indices.
6. Processes data reliably, quickly and regularly.
7. Ensures that this data is fed back to the project team users quickly and accurately.
8. Creates accountability throughout the system, starting at the lowest level.

Figure 10.4 shows how an integrated project control system can work.

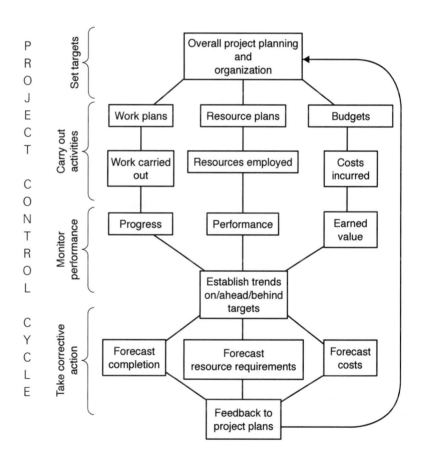

Note the relationship with the project control cycle shown on the left.

FIGURE 10.4: Integrated project control system

PROJECT CHANGES

Changes to the original project specification will probably have the biggest impact on your project. Although we have said that good planning can keep changes to a minimum there may be changes which are unavoidable, or beyond the control of the project team and project manager. Changes can happen for a number of reasons and the most common ones are listed below.

> Changes to the original project specification will probably have the biggest impact of any type of change on your project

SCOPE OF SPECIFICATION CHANGE

This is most likely to happen at the outline design stage as detail is built into the project. The earlier the need for change is identified, the easier and less costly the change will be to implement. But before any changes are implemented you should make sure that the suggested changes are necessary and beneficial.

ERRORS IN OUTLINE SPECIFICATION

This could happen later than the scope or specification change – perhaps during detailed design. Before the change is implemented you would need to establish whether the error is relative to the true objectives and needs of the project. If the specification has been altered for the wrong reasons (such as unnecessary additions) then it may not be legitimate. So, again, you need to check carefully the reasons and true need for the change.

IDENTIFYING A PERFORMANCE IMPROVEMENT

During the detailed design, particularly in a manufacturing environment, a potential improvement in performance may be identified. Before this results in change again, you should go back to the original *objectives and needs* and make sure that the change really is beneficial. Such 'good ideas' of designers can sometimes result in the addition of unnecessary enhancements which over-complicate the end product.

There have been many occasions when products doing more than the user ever needs are so difficult to use that they are never fully put into service. The Ptarmigan field telephone system developed for the US Army is an example. When it had been developed it had so many enhancements that it was too complicated for the American forces' requirements and the cost of the extra performance facilities was wasted. So the danger of 'over design' must be carefully considered before making any changes.

Suggestions for apparently small technical changes can come from a variety of sources, not just the designers. Some of them may be valuable and ought to be considered, but always against the background of their added value weighed against the real needs of the project and the true cost of changes.

CHANGES IN LEGISLATION

This could cover items such as safety requirements and can occur at any stage of the project. Once the necessity for satisfying the legislation has been confirmed then it must be implemented.

The importance of considering potential for legislation at the earliest possible stage should be obvious – and pending legislation as well as existing should be considered.

CONTROL AND FEEDBACK

Whenever it appears that a change is required you should go through a process of checks before it is implemented. A simple control and feedback process is shown in Figure 10.5.

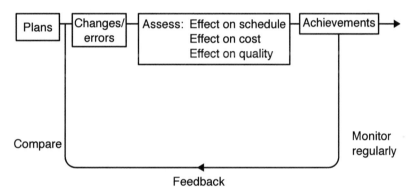

FIGURE 10.5: Control/feedback loop

CHANGE CONTROL

Changes may have different degrees of effect on the project. Three levels could be described:

- *Low level changes*   These will be minor changes which can easily be accommodated and will have little effect on the project.
- *Middle level changes*   These may involve new procedures and routines. They may delay completion or if well handled can be accommodated without really adverse effects on the overall project.
- *High level changes*   These will mean major changes of priorities, costs or the end product. They will require the creation of new behaviours or new sets of values.

We have established that some change is likely during the progress of your project, so it is sensible to plan a method of handling change to ensure minimum disruption and expenditure with maximum effectiveness. You need a means of ensuring that all the required changes are executed as rapidly and precisely as possible; even low level changes must be controlled.

Some change is likely during the progress of your project, so plan a method of handling change

FUNCTIONS OF A CHANGE CONTROL SYSTEM

This will require some sort of change control mechanism. A good system will:

- *Define why*   check the validity of the change
- *Establish what*   define the exact nature of what is to be done
- *Communicate*   ensure that all who need to know are told
- *Ensure accuracy*   the change is carried out correctly
- *Keep records*   the change is recorded and the project records and plans are updated as appropriate
- *Account for effects*   knock-on effects on all other parts of the plan are established and taken into account
- *Have plans*   contingency plans are established
- *Evaluate*   effects are evaluated.

BENEFITS OF CHANGE CONTROL

By considering the necessity of all requests for change you will get into the habit of checking and questioning all such requests. This will make sure that:

- All non-essential changes are rejected
- Inappropriate change decisions are improved upon
- The effects of change will be monitored
- The likely effects of change will be forecast
- Schedules will be adjusted to accommodate change
- Causes and effects of change will be documented for future information
- Effects of change will be evaluated before and after the event.

To limit the possibility of change you should:

- *Freeze* specification at an appropriate stage and only incorporate essential changes thereafter
- Make sure that project objectives are set clearly at the outset
- Consider any changes against the project objectives.

SESSION 10 – EXERCISES WITH YOUR TEAM

OVERVIEW

These exercises are intended to show the importance of monitoring and controlling the project.

EQUIPMENT AND MATERIALS

You will need a flip chart. The team will need paper and pens.

PREPARATION

For Exercise 10.1 you will need to list the 12 examples on one flip chart and draw up the table on another flip chart.

For Exercise 10.2 you will need to write up the question, and on another chart or handout prepare the example 'Change request form'. You will also need another flip chart for brainstorming.

METHOD

Carry out Exercise 10.1 individually or in pairs and then discuss the outcomes. Exercise 10.2 could be carried out first by brainstorming, followed by group discussion.

TIME

Exercise 10.1 will take approximately 15–20 minutes in pairs, plus 10–15 minutes' feedback. Exercise 10.2 should take about 10–15 minutes' brainstorming, plus 10–15 minutes' discussion.

Exercise 10.1

Steps
1. Consider the 12 examples of change identified below.
2. Sort the 12 into the three difference levels by completing the table at the bottom of this display.

Hint

> There are four examples of each of the three *change effect rating levels* identified in this chapter.

Changes
1. New colleague joins the project team
2. Project cutback causes redundancy
3. New product range incorporated
4. Product specification revised slightly
5. The plant is closed down
6. The company loses a major client
7. New target date set
8. New costing procedures established
9. Advanced technologies established
10. Project team restructure during project life
11. Budget for project revised
12. Change of company priorities at senior management levels.

NB There is no sequential ordering within each group.

Low rating

A _____   C _____

B _____   D _____

Medium rating

A _____   C _____

B _____   D _____

High rating

A _____   C _____

B _____   D _____

Exercise 10.2

The example given below is for your own reference; we suggest you only show it to your team if they are having problems with this exercise.

Steps
A change control system can be a valuable tool. A 'change request' form is a useful tool for encouraging formal change requests and monitoring. Under the following headings, discuss the items you consider important, then produce a change request form which you can use for future projects:

Admin information required
Describe change
Reasoning
Effects
Process
Feedback.

Answer
Figure 10.6 on page 116 shows one possible solution.

SUMMARY
Monitoring the project will enable you to see what is happening so you can control it and keep it on course. The project control cycle should be used constantly to monitor and control the project. Many problems can occur, but good monitoring can help you to foresee and forestall many potential problems. Problems can occur in quality cost and time.

CHANGE CONTROL
Change, or requests for change, will have implications for:

- Forecast completion dates and costs
- Established project and activity package budgets
- Manpower and resources plans
- Project team working relationships
- General team motivation.

Different changes will have varying degrees of effect: *low* which can be accommodated easily; *medium* which might cause delay; and *high* which will require a new set of values and dynamic changes.

To establish a complete system for controlling project

```
CHANGE REQUEST

                                              Number _____
                                              Revision _____
                                              Date _____

Project Ref _____

Item affected          Name: _____
                              Activities package: _____
                              Ref no: _____

Change requested by _____

DESCRIPTION OF CHANGE
_____
_____


REASON FOR CHANGE
_____
_____


AREAS/ITEMS AFFECTED BY CHANGE
_____
_____


INITIAL ESTIMATE _____
EXPENDITURE/SAVING*_____
EFFECT ON SCHEDULE _____
FIRM ESTIMATE _____
COMMENTS _____
_____

CHANGE APPROVED/REJECTED*

FOR CONTRACTOR _____      FOR CLIENT_____

            DATE _____            DATE_____

* delete one
```

FIGURE 10.6: Sample change request form

planning and accommodating change, we must also establish a change control information system. A change control system is a means of ensuring that changes required in a project are executed as precisely and rapidly as possible. The total system will also incorporate follow-up controls to ensure smooth change implementation and evaluation of revised performance. The purpose of the different functions in a change control system is to:

1. React quickly to changes essential to safety and success
2. Formalize requests for other changes
3. Forecast cost, time and effect on other activities for management decision
4. Solve disputes with the minimum of conflict
5. Incorporate contingency plans
6. Ensure changes are implemented
7. Maintain costs and evaluate performance

The benefits of incorporating a change control system mean that you can:

- *Assess* the value of proposed change
- *Improve* on the inappropriate change decisions
- *Monitor* the effects of change
- *Forecast* likely effects of change options
- *Adjust* project schedules to accommodate change
- *Document* causes and effects of change
- *Evaluate* effects before and after.

Because of the cyclical nature of project control, the corrective actions which can be established as a direct result of these outputs can be fed back into the system, to carry out the controls shown in Figure 10.7.

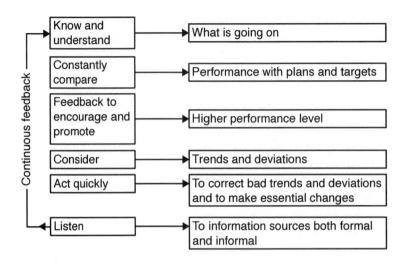

FIGURE 10.7: Effective project control in action

CHAPTER 11

*T*ECHNIQUES FOR MONITORING AND CONTROL 1: TIME

KEY LEARNING POINTS

■ Know methods for controlling time
■ Know outcomes of using the methods

WHY DO WE NEED TO CONTROL TIME?

Project management techniques can be used in a great variety of circumstances. Projects can include topics as diverse as putting on a major sporting event to designing and building a motorway. Although it is important that any project should be completed on time, within budget and to specification, some projects are more time sensitive than others:

Project management techniques can be used in a great variety of circumstances

> A good example of a time-sensitive project is the Olympic Games. Although it happens every four years it is in a different venue, involves different personnel and budgets will vary according to the sponsorship available and the willingness (or ability) of the host nation to put in funds.

Planning the Games begins even before the host country is nominated, but once that has been agreed things begin in earnest. Everything must be covered from building or refurbishing the stadia, organizing accommodation for athletes, officials and spectators to training the first aiders (often including many volunteers).

Certain items are set and do not change from year to year, but in some years new events have been added. In addition, each host country adds its own personal touches particularly in the opening ceremonies and other peripheral events. During the course of the Games weather can affect the time of heats and other unpredictable things can happen. But whatever these changes are, two facts remain fixed – the start date and the finish date. No matter what problems and difficulties arise, these dates must be kept.

You can probably easily think of many other situations where time is the crucial factor – from launching a new product to delivering a demonstration at a conference. The situation is, that whatever problems arise you cannot be late!

To achieve this delivery certain things must be in place, and during the progress of the project certain actions are crucial. During the rest of this chapter we will look at these in more detail.

THREATS TO MAINTAINING PROJECT SCHEDULES

A few years ago, a well-known firm of engineering consultants published a list of the major reasons why companies fall behind in project schedules, incurring time and/or cost penalties. Several of these reasons were a direct result of not responding positively enough to change. They were:

1. *Project plan was too rigid to adapt to inevitable changes* This was a potential problem where too-detailed planning was developed at an early stage in the project – with a resultant reluctance to waste time changing plans or networks.
2. *The effects of necessary project changes were not fully evaluated* Overcoming this is one of the major purposes of the change control system (which we looked at in Chapter 10).

3. *Consciously putting back the original completion date through uncontrolled change*   This is using change as a reason for delay rather than rescheduling around it as much as possible.
4. *Underestimating the impact of change*   In degree, this would be considered as between reasons 2 and 3 above. The changes and their effects have been acknowledged, with efforts made to adapt the project, but without enough detailed analysis to identify some of the indirect effects.

In any dynamic systems, especially those involving new and innovative techniques, change will happen naturally as detail becomes progressively more complex. Thus, in managing and controlling projects, the emphasis should be on monitoring and, as far as possible, predicting change within an established control system, rather than resisting or restricting change.

WHAT PROBLEMS CAN ARISE?

The problems which can affect the time of projects are varied, but we will consider in this chapter the most common ones and the ways in which you can avoid or overcome them. The first thing you would see as the result of a problem is the effect it has. The cause may not be immediately obvious. So, for example, you may discover that something which should have been done has not; you may find that a task which should have been completed in two weeks has taken three. But initially the reasons why are not evident.

The first thing you would see as the result of a problem is the effect it has

Frequently the reasons for the problem are obvious (someone off sick, failure of supplier to deliver materials), but occasionally this is not the case. Where the problem has no obvious cause you will need to carry out a problem-solving exercise to find out why. This may require the help of some or all of the team, but should be done as soon as possible to ensure that the root cause is found and corrective action taken to avoid repetition of the problem.

EFFECTS ON QUALITY

Trying to save time because problems have caused delays can sometimes result in producing a process or product which is inferior to the original specification. This does not always have to be the case – but is usually the easiest or most obvious solution and so a very tempting route to take. But it should never be taken without going right back to the project objectives and ensuring that these are not compromised.

EFFECTS ON COST

The effects of time problems on cost are as many and varied as there are problems – but almost always a problem will result in a rise in the cost. To solve the problem work may have to be carried out by alternative suppliers, additional resources will have to be brought in or overtime paid.

The effects are simple – the solutions are more problematic. If there is no additional budget available, other means of solving the problem will have to be found.

COMPANY COMMITMENT

Different functions in an organization will invariably to be involved in any project. Considering the various inter-relationships between different functions it is essential that there is positive support from senior management. This does not mean the abdication of their responsibility, but the commitment to put in place those things which are necessary for good project management to take place. This can be summarized in diagrammatic form and is shown in Figure 11.1.

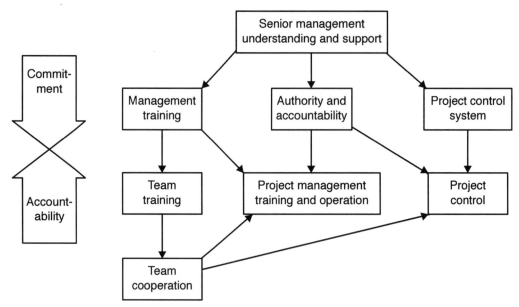

FIGURE 11.1: Company commitment to project control

Someone is accountable for every activity that has to take place to complete the project. That person or those people must also be committed and empowered to do what is necessary to achieve this. That does not mean that they work alone – good communication is an essential for the success of any project team (we considered this earlier in Chapter 4).

WILL IT BE COMPLETED ON TIME?

Going back to the example of planning the Olympic Games which we mentioned earlier, we said that it had to be completed on time but did not say how. Obviously, good initial planning is essential. For a project as large as this it has to be broken down into many sub-projects, each with its own team and project manager.

Although the sub-project teams could meet regularly, it would not be feasible for the whole project team to meet – so the sub-project managers would meet on a regular basis to share their progress and exchange updates and ideas.

Many of the items which have to be planned can be based on past experience or known facts. For example, for activities such as the timing of the medal ceremonies the previous Games would be timed in fine detail and this information fed into the system. But other steps can be taken to minimize the risks or build in back-up procedures.

CONTINGENCIES AND 'WHAT IF'S'

Certain things cannot be measured precisely. That is where contingency planning and 'what if' scenarios come in. Wherever an activity includes an element of unknown, an analysis needs to be undertaken which looks at the following issues:

1. What are the known facts?
2. What are the unknowns?
3. What could happen?
4. What is the best/worst case scenario?
5. What contingencies do we need to build in to cover this?

This then gives additional information which can be built into the planning. It may take the form of extra time for the most high-risk activities, or it could mean having additional resources on stand by with additional budget to cover these.

CONTINGENCIES AND CRITICALITY

The next crucial stage in the time planning is to draw up a *critical path network* and look carefully at the activities on the critical path. If any of the critical activities are high risk, wherever possible you should look for ways of minimizing this risk or moving them off the critical path.

Certain things cannot be measured precisely. That is where contingency planning and 'what if' scenarios come in

If any of the critical activities are high risk, wherever possible you should look for ways of minimizing this risk or moving them off the critical path

Again, this could be achieved by having additional resources or back-up systems. This may be expensive, but if the items are critical it could be justified. For example:

> If the completion of a new hotel for the athletes to stay in is on the critical path – what happens if it is not ready on time? What could you do to minimize this effect?
>
> To find out the worst possible situation you could carry out a 'what if' scenario, find out how many rooms you would be short of and try to book these elsewhere. Or you could put additional resources into the building, so giving it more time and moving it off the critical path.

The best solutions can be effected when forward planning and constant monitoring alert you to the problems or potential problems in good time. In drawing up your project plan you would normally build in milestones. These are points at which key activities are completed or delivered. In a time-centred project you may wish to build in more milestones to enable you to check the achievement of key steps on a more frequent basis.

This process of planning including 'what if's', contingencies and criticality is only the beginning; it is during the progress of the project that they provide the basis of control.

PROGRESS MONITORING

During the progress of the project you can use the plan and the monitoring techniques discussed in Chapter 10 to control the project. If the most important factor in your project is delivery on time, then this is the first thing you must check on a regular basis. You may choose to do this at given milestones or on a regular timed basis; the time interval depending on the overall scope of the project. There is no hard and fast rule for how often this should be. Most experienced project managers find that it will depend on the overall length of the project, the current stage and activities being undertaken along with their confidence in and experience of the individual or individuals involved at any one time. So at some stages the manager may not check progress for a week or more, at others he or she will be monitoring daily.

You will find that with some suppliers or team members you can agree a delivery date and it will always happen on time. With others you may need to chase them, so when the order is agreed make a note in your system to ring them to chase it up a certain time before delivery is due. How often and with whom you need to do this will be learned through experience. Until you have that experience or know the suppliers and team members, assume the worst and have a system for chasing up!

YOUR SYSTEM

It is helpful if you have a system for 'triggering' your involvement when necessary, for example, a system of bring forward files into which you put notes of things to be done that day. This could also be done in a diary or time management system. There is no one 'correct' method – the method you use must suit you and the way you work. Look at other people's systems and off the shelf ones which you can buy, then adapt them to fit your needs. It is no use having a set of bring forward files on your desk if most of your project takes place out of the office. Neither is it any good writing things in a diary which you never look at.

Again in the interests of good communication, it should be agreed what information is kept centrally and it is usually the responsibility of the project manager to make sure this is always done. It is useful to have a system for keeping a master file for each of your projects or sub-projects. In the file should be kept a copy of all key documents including:

- CPN, the original plan plus regular updates
- Project feasibility study or proposal
- Budgets (there is more about this in Chapter 13)
- Important correspondence with the customer or champion (internal or external)
- Important correspondence with all suppliers
- Meeting reports
- Change requests
- Progress reports
- Other control forms
- Any compliance information (essential requirements).

If one file gets too full, split it and keep some sections (for example, budgets) in another file. All files, however, should be kept together and all accessible to other team members. If the project manager goes sick someone else should be able to read the file and very quickly pick up the project.

PROGRESS REPORTING

It is often necessary to produce formal reports for your manager or for a customer. Again this should be designed to suit the needs of the project. There is no point in writing lengthy reports in beautiful prose if no one will ever read them. But on the other hand, it is important that the progress of the project is tracked on a regular basis and then recorded in some form.

Some project managers prefer to produce information in chart or table form and it is sometimes quicker for others to assimilate visually. In the interest of good communications you must record information and share it with the rest of the project team somehow. It will greatly assist understanding and sharing if there is an agreed standard for doing this, preferably agreed between the team members to suit their needs rather than imposed upon them.

Many computer packages will automatically produce reports provided you update the information on project progress regularly. Once the plan and detailed project information have been input at the outset it is usually easy to update the progress. The computerized method has the great advantage that by updating one thing the system can be set to update all affected areas and then produce reports in a variety of formats.

It is important that the progress of the project is tracked on a regular basis and then recorded in some form

SESSION 11 – EXERCISES WITH YOUR TEAM

OVERVIEW
These exercises will enable you to discuss effects of change on your projects and methods for alleviating or eliminating time problems. These will be in the form of guidelines or an action plan.

EQUIPMENT AND MATERIALS
You will require a flip chart.

PREPARATION
Write the four phases given in Exercise 11.1 onto the chart. On another chart write up the questions for Exercise 11.2 and decide on a project which is time sensitive to use in the exercise (past, present or future) and known by the team members if possible. Then write the title of this on top of the chart.

If you cannot use a company example there is an alternative exercise given after 11.2. If you are using this one then you will need to write out the information on handouts before the session.

METHOD

Brainstorming and discussion.

TIME

Exercise 11.1 will take approximately 20–30 minutes; exercise 11.2 20 minutes.

Exercise 11.1

Steps

1. By brainstorming or discussion, produce two or three examples of 'legitimate changes' which could occur at each of these project phases:
   - Phase 6 Planning
   - Phase 7 Engineering design
   - Phase 8 Purchasing and procurement
   - Phase 10 Commissioning
2. Now look at the examples and consider what effect these would have on the ability to complete a project on time. Discuss this and make notes by each example.
3. Finally, discuss solutions to overcome these problems and consider how you might implement these to avoid future problems. Note these ideas on another flip chart.
4. Ask one or two team members to make a note of these points and produce an action plan or set of guidelines (maximum one side of A4) for circulation among all team members.

Exercise 11.2

Referring to your chosen project answer and note the following questions:

1. Why was it time sensitive?
2. What, if any, factors were flexible (for example cost)?

List the problems this project had. Now think about these problems and discuss the following:

1. How were they resolved?
2. Could they have been better handled?
3. What lessons could you learn?

Alternative Exercise 11.2

If you cannot use a company example use the following:

1. Stage 4 produces problems with materials procurement – preferred supplier cannot conform to specification.
2. Stage 5 – materials problem still not resolved.
3. Stage 12 throws up problems with one machine on line producing out of spec work. Takes 10 days to fix.
4. Stage 16 – literature print problems due to late pictures of production models.

Exercise 11.2A

How would you tackle the problems above? Assume budgets have been set for the whole project and cannot be added to, also that time is critical as the conference cannot be moved.

Exercise 11.2B

Assuming the start and finish dates are fixed, what could you have done within your original plan to minimize the possibility or alleviate the effects of such problems?

Answer
There is no 'correct' solution to this scenario. Work within the normal parameters of your company's or your own experience, but you should draw on the guidance in the preceding chapter to help you.

SUMMARY

WHY DO WE NEED TO CONTROL TIME?
In projects where time is a crucial factor we need to plan time for each activity carefully, then monitor the schedule step by step throughout the project. In this way we can see any deviations to the schedule at an early stage and take corrective action quickly.

THREATS TO MAINTAINING SCHEDULES
The main threats are:

- Project plan too rigid to adapt to changes
- Effects of necessary changes not fully evaluated
- Completion date put back due to *uncontrolled* changes
- Underestimating the effects of change.

PROBLEMS

The main problems caused by poor project time control are:

- Increased costs
- Reduction in quality.

Problems can be overcome by:

- Careful monitoring and control
- Timely action
- Negotiation where appropriate
- Empowering the project manager
- Company commitment.

COMPLETING ON TIME

This can be helped by good initial planning which includes 'what if' scenarios and contingencies. The monitoring and control will need to take especial account of the critical activities when progress is being monitored.

There needs to be a good reporting structure to ensure that anyone who needs to know what is happening is kept informed. This should take account of informal as well as formal communications networks.

CHAPTER 12

*T*ECHNIQUES FOR MONITORING AND CONTROL 2: RESOURCES

KEY LEARNING POINTS
■ Know methods for controlling resources
■ Know the outcomes of using these methods

WHY CONTROL RESOURCES?

Resources are probably the most important factor in the successful completion of any project. Resources can include equipment, facilities and personnel. In this chapter we will be concentrating on the personnel aspects of resources. This can mean members of the project team, or suppliers and sub-contractors.

    When we talked about the importance of planning in earlier chapters, we considered how to plan the resources required for a

> Resources are probably the most important factor in the successful completion of any project

project. We also said that a project can be driven by its available resources. So you can plan a project based on time and put in as much resource as you need to complete on time. Or, when resources are finite, you can consider the available resources and plan your project to utilize these most effectively.

If you have produced a resource based plan this will often mean that you do not have access to further resources – either because of availability or cost constraints. In this case it is essential that the resources you have are monitored and controlled to ensure that you are making the most efficient use of them.

There are activities in a project which depend on completion of preceding activities before they can begin. In the simple example of building a wall which we used earlier, you cannot begin bricklaying until the bricks have been delivered. But if you have only one bricklayer you do not want them wasting time waiting for bricks to arrive when they could be working on another job on another site! So it is essential that you plan their availability to follow immediately after the delivery of the bricks – no sooner. You must, however, make sure that the bricks (another resource) are delivered on time otherwise you are wasting your bricklayer resource.

In more complex projects, similar situations often arise. The more complex the project, the more likely it is that one resource can be wasted or mis-timed and will have to knock-on effect and upset later plans. It is, therefore, essential that your project is monitored to control this.

SHARED RESOURCES

Resources shared between more than one project need to be taken into account at the planning stage

It is often the case that resources will be shared between more than one project. Even members of your project team may have other functions to perform outside the scope of your project. It is certain that freelance personnel and sub-contractors will have other work involvements.

There may be occasions when schedules need to be re-arranged to utilize resources when they are available. If resources are shared, that it, not exclusive to that project, then planning must take account of this and contingency plans may be needed.

EFFECTS OF RESOURCES ON QUALITY, COST AND TIME

As with all aspects of managing a project, any changes to the plan have the potential for affecting all the three points of the project management triangle.

EFFECTS ON QUALITY

Effects on quality are not straightforward to assess and may be difficult to quantify objectively. There is no doubt that it is important to have the right resource for the job in terms of manpower and equipment. Personnel trained to the required standard and with the appropriate experience will be required to carry out each task. They will also require the right tools or equipment to perform correctly. This means setting the requirements against the objectives of the project, and illustrates the importance of knowing the specification and objectives at the earliest stage. There is little point in employing resources who are over-qualified and will therefore cost more than is justifiable; but if you are not sure of the standards required, how can you judge this?

You may begin a project with certain assumptions, but during the progress of the project changes or unforeseen circumstances could result in these requirements changing. If this change means that the available resources are no longer sufficiently qualified to carry out the task, how can this be solved?

First, the change control process we discussed in Chapter 10 must be invoked to ensure that the change is necessary and beneficial. This must then be carefully compared with the specification. Finally, any possible effects on quality can be identified and the requirements to maintain quality ascertained. Within this process, the project manager can make sure that quality issues are addressed before the project fails to meet specification and resources adjusted accordingly.

This process may involve additional cost or time – and these items must be brought into the change control process and the priorities agreed.

EFFECTS ON COST

It is obvious that more resources will incur more cost. But if the penalties for late delivery are high, then this cost could be offset against the overall success of the project or penalty costs for failing to deliver.

EFFECTS ON TIME

Lack of resources can lengthen the time of the project. Adding additional resources may reduce time, but only where activities can be run in parallel or where more than one resource can work on one activity at the same time. Thus, in our example of building a wall, increasing the number of bricklayers might shorten the time, but if it was a restricted site, too many could get in the way and even slow the building work down!

RESOURCE SMOOTHING

By planning manpower during the planning phase of the project, the project manager can identify the times when specific resources will be required. Sometimes, smaller numbers of people will be needed; at other times, all available manpower will be required. It will not always be possible to redeploy these 'spare' personnel during the slack times. While the plan can indicate when and what the maximum requirement is, it may not be possible to redeploy the spare manpower during the slack times without risking them being unavailable when required.

Sometimes, therefore, the spare personnel should be kept on the same job, carrying out non-essential work, although strictly speaking they are not required. This may not be as cost-effective as moving them, but will ensure their availability for times when they are really needed. This is known as *resource smoothing*. Although it actually takes place at the planning stage, it does give the project manager some flexibility during the other phases of the project.

By planning manpower during the planning phase of the project, the project manager can identify the times when specific resources will be required

OVERCOMING RESOURCE PROBLEMS

Resource problems can sometimes prove to be the most difficult to overcome. Problems can be due to too much or too little resource or to changes in personnel.

Resource problems can sometimes prove to be the most difficult to overcome

ONLY ONE AVAILABLE RESOURCE

If parts of the project require one particular 'expert' and they have limited availability, this can be a major hurdle. The only way to tackle this is by good planning and communication. Steps you can take are:

1. Plan time requirements and when these are to take place as far in advance as possible.
2. Communicate these and agree dates and deliverables.
3. Monitor to keep project on schedule so these dates are not lost.
4. Monitor and communicate changes to requirements as soon as possible to give time to negotiate.

TOO MANY RESOURCES

If you have areas of work where many people are required and other areas where few are needed, consider the resource smoothing we described earlier. Again, this requires good planning and it can be helped by employing flexible and multi-skilled workers wherever possible.

RESOURCE CHANGES

Sometimes key personnel may fall ill or leave during the progress of a project. If they are leaving, a good team atmosphere and good communications will make it more likely that you will have reasonable warning. This can give you more time to find a replacement.

Sickness is unplanned and, therefore, more difficult to overcome. A flexible workforce can help, but not always. Contingency planning on crucial areas could mean that you have back-up systems. Carrying out a 'what if' can show you the worst case scenario at that time and may give you information to help you decide whether to move resources, reschedule or put in more budget to overcome the problem.

SESSION 12 – EXERCISES WITH YOUR TEAM

OVERVIEW

This exercise will give you an opportunity to discuss resourcing with your team.

EQUIPMENT AND MATERIALS

You will require a flip chart.

PREPARATION

Look back at the activity to plan the resources allocation for a project which you carried out in Exercise 8.1. You will need to write up the outcomes of Exercise 8.1 on the flip chart or a handout. You should write out the questions on another chart.

If you have not got the results of Exercise 8.1 or do not wish to use them, there is an alternative exercise which you can use.

METHOD

Group discussion.

TIME

Approximately 20–30 minutes.

Exercise 12.1

Steps

Look back at Exercise 8.1. Using the information you produced, consider the following questions:

1. How flexible are the resources if planned at this stage?
   - Is there a way I could carry out some resource smoothing or provide more flexibility?
   - Is there any part of the project which relies entirely on one key resource?
   - If so, why is this? Is this necessary?
   - Is there any way I could reduce the risk of this reliance?

Discuss each question with your team and note the answers.

Alternative Exercise 12.1

If Exercise 8.1 did not produce a manpower plan which you could use as a basis for the exercise above, use the information below.

Equipment, materials and preparation

In addition to the questions for Exercise 12.1 on a flip chart, you will need to produce a handout with the information below:

Activity	Duration for 1 unit of resource (days)	Resources available	Potential problems
Plan project	6	Self only	
Cost project	4	Self + suppliers or Tom	
Order materials	2	Self or Tom	

Activity	Duration for 1 unit of resource (days)	Resources available	Potential problems
Sanction order	$\frac{1}{2}$	Joe	
Wait/Delivery bricks Wait/Delivery mortar	3 to 6	Bloggs & Co or Gibson & Son	
Dig foundations	8	John, Fred or Alan	
Bricklaying	8	Alan	
Mix mortar	8	Jim, Fred or Alan	

SUMMARY

WHY CONTROL RESOURCES?

Resources are probably the most important factor in the success of a project. They can include equipment, facilities and personnel and the personnel aspects are the most important for the project manager to control.

Some plans are *resources based*, that is, they are driven by available resources.

It is easy, especially in complex projects, to waste or mis-time resources, so monitoring throughout is essential to control resources and use them most effectively.

SHARED RESOURCES

Where resources are shared between more than one project or a number of activities, it is sometimes necessary to develop the other aspects of the project to utilize the resources most effectively.

EFFECTS OF POOR RESOURCES MANAGEMENT

Lack of resources can lengthen a project, so upsetting the schedule.

Having to add resources will incur more cost, so affecting the project budget.

Inadequate or inappropriate resources can adversely affect the quality of the project outcomes.

RESOURCE SMOOTHING

Planning the utilization of resources so that you do not have resources idle at some times and overstretched at others is known as *resources smoothing*. It is best built in at the planning stage, although changes during the project may make it necessary at other times.

PROBLEMS

Resources problems are often the most difficult to overcome. Good planning far in advance can help, as can regular monitoring and good communications.

A flexible workforce and contingency planning are also effective means to help better resource utilization in times of problem.

CHAPTER 13

TECHNIQUES FOR MONITORING AND CONTROL 3: COSTS

KEY LEARNING POINT

■ **Know methods of controlling**

WHY MONITOR COSTS?

This might seem a stupid question. But consider how many projects are allowed to run over budget when simple control techniques could have prevented much of the overspend. To enable the project manager to control costs it is essential for two things to happen:

■ There must be a robust project budget set at the planning stage
■ This must be continually monitored throughout the progress of the project.

An inaccurate budget is a poor control tool.

We looked earlier at a number of projects as examples of ones which went spectacularly over budget. Although only a few project managers will be involved in projects of such a scale, the lessons are worth noting for all of us. For example, we came to the conclusion with the Concorde project that the main problems were due to the

An inaccurate budget is a poor control tool

uncertainty of the end product as there was a predominance of research and development. However, the planning stage should have taken more account of past lessons and planned contingencies.

Monitoring the budget will enable the project manager to carry out two major tasks:

- Predict and control cash flow
- Take measures in time to stop the budget escalating.

Good initial planning and regular monitoring can enable the project manager to cope with changes of plan. Costs cannot be seen in isolation – time and resources affect costs and so must be monitored too.

Having looked in some detail at the planning stage and budgeting, the project manager should know how to plan a budget which is robust and so provides a sound basis for monitoring and controlling the costs.

ACCOUNTABILITY

Awareness of costs and accountability for control of costs should be the responsibility of *all* team members

We looked in detail in Chapter 4 at the role of different members of the project team. Within the team there may be an individual whose prime task is to keep track of financial matters; but the project manager usually has ultimate responsibility for the project budget. However, awareness of costs and accountability for control of costs should be the responsibility of *all* team members. This awareness should include the knowledge of the time allocated for all his or her own tasks and the cost of materials and resources.

Time delays and the requirement for additional resources are major reasons for cost escalation, and these are within the control of many team members. Obviously team members need to be given authority to make some decisions – it is unrealistic for every minor detail to have to be cleared through the project manager. But with that authority they must be given the information they need to understand all implications of their decisions and accountability for the outcomes. It is up to the project manager how far this is extended and will likely depend on the experience of the individual team members and also the scope of the project.

Monitoring and overall control can be helped if invoices and other costs are coded or are allocated to specific cost centres (we looked at coding for activity packages in Chapter 9). The project manager or those responsible at activity package level can then check invoices against any cost centre to ensure that they are on target. If actual expenditure is checked against budgeted expenditure at regular intervals within the reporting period of the time-phased budget then potential overspends can be flagged. Costs expected but not realized can also be seen.

SHOULD BUDGETS BE ALTERED?

The budget is the tool which the project manager uses to monitor and control the costs of the project. But being realistic it is likely that project plans, and therefore budgets, will change due to unforeseen circumstances. No matter how well the project has been planned, we have seen how changes can happen. So plans must be flexible enough to take account of *legitimate* alterations. Any potential changes must be closely scrutinized and justified. We should *not* change budgets to compensate for poor project management at planning or execution stages.

ARE BUDGET ALTERATIONS JUSTIFIED?

Each project manager and each project will have different criteria, but there are a number of situations where alterations are usually justifiable. The most likely ones are:

- In development projects new activities may have to be added where unknown or unexpected items have to be inserted. These should be dealt with by adding additional coded cost centres. This will enable easy monitoring of the new activities.
- In a time-phased budget where activities alter from the original plan such as the earlier purchase of items of equipment. This may show the movement of costs, but the overall costs will remain the same. This could produce short-term cash flow problems but not increased costs.

RE-ALLOCATION OF FUNDS

As we have seen before, it may sometimes be necessary to move part of the costs from one time period to another. But the funds are still to be used for the same items or activities. In other circumstances, it may be necessary to re-allocate funds from one item to another. If increased costs in one area require budget revisions, savings may have to be made elsewhere so funds can be re-allocated.

Although not desirable, this is a technique often used by project managers to keep the project within its overall budget but take account of unforeseen circumstances. It should rarely be necessary to carry out major revisions of a project time-phased budget, although in a long-term project it may become necessary on a small number of occasions.

CASH FLOW FORECASTING

Cash flow forecasting can help to overcome the problems of moving activities and purchases. The cash in and cash out of the project can be monitored by drawing a graph similar to the one shown in Figure 13.1. By taking a milestone at any given time (shown by the vertical line on the graph) any discrepancy can easily be seen – in this case, a negative cash flow of £50 000. This may be unavoidable, but good cash flow forecasting could enable the project manager to move the timing of other costs to help the cash flow. Or, at least, to arrange suitable loan facilities. Cash flow is most important in smaller organizations. A large corporation could carry a negative flow of £50 000, but it could cause major problems for a small one.

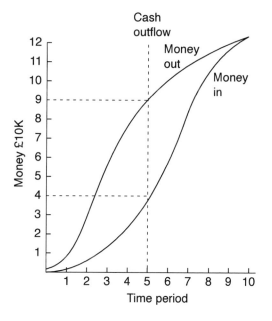

FIGURE 13.1: Cash flow forecast chart

EFFECTS OF COST ON QUALITY AND TIME

The saying 'You get what you pay for' is certainly true of project management. Cost cutting frequently results in poor quality or longer timescales. Where budgets are not monitored carefully, there can be overspend at the early stages of the project and the result may be to delay the project by cutting resources later to reduce the specification of the end product.

Frequently the timescales and quality have to be maintained and it is the budget that suffers. Causes of major problems are rarely simple and sometimes all three – quality, cost and time – are casualties.

COMPANY LED PRIORITIES

For any particular industry there are standards set for quality and safety. For any specific project senior management should review the objects and needs of the project in relation to these standards and consider how they compare in relation to the marketplace and this product. Revised criteria can then be established which will maintain the priority standards but within a cost-effective framework. This needs to be done at the outset, and the designers, engineers and other project team members informed or trained in their implementation.

It is sometimes possible to design a product which requires more initial input but less maintenance, therefore reducing overall costs. In the motor industry, for example, improvements in reliability have meant more expensive components but less warranty claims. In the aviation industry, safety standards are exceedingly high, but because of market pressures airlines are constantly reviewing requirements for servicing and refurbishment to find the most cost-effective procedures but still satisfy the safety criteria.

CHANGE CONTROL

We have already discovered that early estimates do not usually take account of changes to the design and scope of a project. Some changes are therefore highly likely and we have discussed in Chapter 10 the need for a change control system.

COST ESCALATION

Cost escalation can be defined as, 'The difference between final cost (or latest forecast) and the original estimate'. Cost escalation is a feature of many projects. A study of the published data on project cost overruns shows that 90 per cent of projects exceed their budget and in most cases poor project planning and control is at the root of this. Also, since sub-contractors could try to get loose specifications which they can exploit if project management is not professional.

In the Dungeness B reactor project cost overrun amounted to £500 million above the original estimate of £111 million – about the same percentage cost escalation as the Concorde project. How does cost escalation, especially on this massive scale, come about? There are a number of key factors which contribute to cost escalation.

INEFFICIENCY

Loose project control or lack of effective planning can cause cost escalation. Thus, the prevention of inefficiency should be very much within the project leader's control. With tight initial specifications, regular monitoring and stated responsibilities and deadlines, there is seldom an acceptable excuse for inefficiency.

INFLATION

Inflation, especially on the longer-term project, is very difficult to predict. As we have seen in the 1980s with the fluctuating value of oil, inflation can change dramatically over an extended period of time, against all predictions. A percentage can be added to allow for inflation but again, in the longer-term project, this is rarely accurate or effective.

For projects involving foreign currencies in any way, exchange rates as well as inflation can create cost escalation. Companies who trade abroad regularly may have techniques for dealing with this. Others should take professional advice at the time of the project.

LACK OF INFORMATION WHEN ESTIMATING

This situation is quite likely to arise, especially on the innovative type of project. Having to estimate in detail before or during the specification of a project will tend to encourage approximate estimations. This will lead to contingency costing relative to the degree of uncertainty of the final project specification, giving a high possibility of inaccuracy.

CHANGES TO THE CONTRACT

Unless carefully controlled, contract changes can weaken the management and budgetary control of a project. Changes to the contract will inevitably cause changes to the project requirements. This must be taken account of in the project management system so that the full implications and costs of the changes are evaluated before being implemented.

POOR COORDINATION

This can be the result of a lack of positive management and teamwork within a company or can occur where many different suppliers and sub-contractors are involved in a project. It can also be caused by a mix of public and private accountability, where initial objectives become clouded and extra specifications and require-ments are included for 'political' reasons. Poor coordination reduces the possibility of having effective project controls, potentially leading to cost escalation.

Although these factors can cause cost escalation, their effects can all be controlled to some extent (apart from inflation, perhaps). This control can come from the project manager in the first instance, but also from the client and/or senior management.

WHAT IF THE CONTROLS DON'T WORK?

It might seem a bit defeatist to suggest that in the end the controls we have been considering might fail, but occasionally a combination of factors could cause irretrievable damage, as the following example shows:

The project to develop the Advanced Passenger Train (APT) by British Rail was delayed considerably by a combination of factors: design errors, labour problems and poor implementation.

The problems with the design of the tilting carriages which would enable the train to corner at high speed were never completely solved and ultimately the train was withdrawn.

Although conceived by the new British Rail research organization, the project was better supported by the Ministry of Transport than the British Rail Board – so the prerequisites for effective control were not in place.

The ultimate decision was not entirely based on cost factors, but illustrates a number of areas where initial planning, company commitment and project control were at fault.

GO/NO GO DECISIONS

Projects can reach stages where it may be necessary to decide whether to proceed or abort. It is most cost-effective to abort at the earliest stage possible, when least expenditure has been incurred. The further into the project you are, the more costly it is to abort. At a later stage so much as been invested in the project that it can become too late to abort. Particularly when a company's public image and reputation rely on completion, the decision to carry on will be made as much on the desire to gain at least some benefit for

It may be necessary to decide whether to proceed or abort – in the end it may be politics or prestige rather than cost which makes the decision

all the work and cost! For this reason alone, constant monitoring and control is worthwhile.

Nonetheless, it may occasionally be necessary to consider aborting the project. To do this sensibly, realistic estimates must be in place, or it must be possible for them to be put in place for future expenditure. The decisions should be based on:

- The rate of return of the project
- Forecasts of costs to and at completion.

In the final analysis it may be politics or prestige rather than cost which makes the decision!

SESSION 13 – EXERCISES WITH YOUR TEAM

OVERVIEW
The results of Exercise 13.1 could be used to produce a checklist or job aid to help with future cost control.

EQUIPMENT AND MATERIALS
You will require a flip chart.

PREPARATION
Produce your own notes from the information in this chapter to answer the questions and to use as a checklist at the end of the exercise. Write this on a flip chart for reference later. Also write the questions for each exercise on separate flip charts.

Exercise 13.3 requires you first to think back to considering the budget. You may wish to re-read the summary of Chapter 9 to remind you of the planning issues relating to cost control before you carry out the next exercise.

For Exercise 13.4 you may want to draw up a list of sample documents like those given at the end of the exercise as handouts for a 'starter' in the exercise.

METHOD
Both Exercises 13.1 and 13.2 use brainstorming and discussion with the whole team.

TIME
Exercise 13 should take about 10 minutes brainstorming, plus 10

minutes discussion. Exercises 13.2 and 13.3 should each take about 10 minutes brainstorming plus 20 minutes discussion. Exercise 13.4 will probably take about 20–30 minutes discussion, plus follow up work by individuals later.

Exercise 13.1

Steps

1. Ask your team the following question, then brainstorm and note the answers: 'What do you think are the benefits of monitoring the cost of a project?'
2. When you finish brainstorming, consider each of the points and discuss their importance.
3. You could check the list against the points made in this chapter, then discuss how you could collectively ensure that all information relevant to monitoring costs is collected by the team and shared with the appropriate members.
4. Make a note of the main points. Ask a team member to write this up as a handout for your project management training folder.

Exercise 13.2

Steps

1. From any experience you have had in the past list situations which have occurred which caused major alterations to the budget during the life of a project.
2. For each of the situations note briefly the cause (arrived at by discussion and consensus).
3. Discuss what could have been done to:
   - Prevent the problem arising in the first place.
   - Solve or reduce the impact of it once it had occurred.

Exercise 13.3

Steps

1. Initially brainstorm and list on a flip chart the answer to this question: 'Using the outcomes of the previous two exercises, as a team list the possible cost control mechanisms you could put in place for your current or future projects'.

2. Then discuss each idea. The following questions will guide you in the discussion:
   - Is it realistic?
   - Is it practical?
   - How will it help?
   - Who should be responsible?
   - What information/interfaces does it require?
3. Finally, make up a checklist of cost control mechanisms and responsibilities which you can use as a future reminder. Work on it as a team to reach consensus, but task one or two members with writing it up as a handout for future use.

Note: It is important that all the team agrees and the list should not be used as an excuse to pass on blame!

Exercise 13.4

Overview
We would not wish to encourage the production of more paperwork than is necessary. However, some system for recording information is an essential part of project control. In the case of financial controls this can be particularly useful.

Steps
1. With your team, look back at the control mechanisms you agreed on in Exercise 13.3 above. Brainstorm to produce a list of documents which you might use to help with this.

Hint

Below we give examples of a few which might be useful. You can use these to start off your thinking, or as prompts if you run out of ideas.

---

2. You can use this list to produce the appropriate documents. Each team member or pair should be given the task to draw up a form for one aspect of budgetary control. These should be brought back to the next meeting for discussion and refinement. Examples of control forms are given in Figure 13.2.

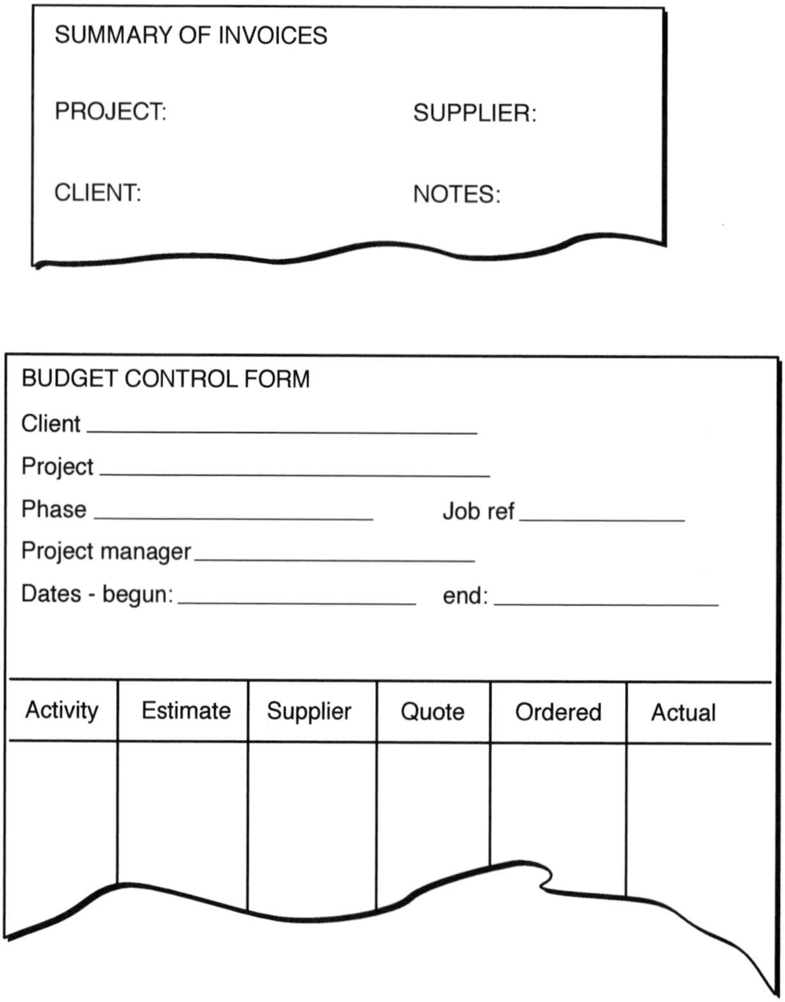

SUMMARY OF INVOICES

PROJECT: SUPPLIER:

CLIENT: NOTES:

BUDGET CONTROL FORM

Client _____

Project _____

Phase _____   Job ref _____

Project manager_____

Dates - begun: _____   end: _____

Activity	Estimate	Supplier	Quote	Ordered	Actual

FIGURE 13.2

SUMMARY

WHY MONITOR COSTS?

To enable project costs to be monitored there must be a robust budget. Monitoring will enable the project manager to:

- Predict and control cash flow
- Take measures in time to stop budget escalation.

ACCOUNTABILITY

All team members have a responsibility for monitoring and controlling budgets. In this way cost escalation may be avoided.

BUDGET ALTERATIONS

Alterations to the budget should be made only if essential. Steps should be taken to avoid this wherever possible. Funds may be re-allocated within the budget if circumstances make this necessary.

EFFECTS ON QUALITY AND TIME

Cost can affect the quality and time of the project, so controlling cost will have benefits on quality and time as well as funds.

COST ESCALATION

Cost escalation can be caused by:

- Inefficiency
- Inflation
- Lack of information when estimating
- Changes to the contract
- Poor coordination.

Good planning and control can minimize cost and avoid escalation.

CHAPTER 14

THE COMPUTER IN PROJECT MANAGEMENT

KEY LEARNING POINTS

- Understand how the computer can help manage projects
- Understand the limitations of computers in project management
- Guidelines for selecting computer software

INTRODUCTION

Although most of what is described in this chapter can also apply to mainframe computers, it is written with PC users in mind. Most PCs are powerful enough to run the project management software currently needed for basic project management. Where a mainframe is to be used, specialist IT or systems personnel will need to be involved in any decisions on the use of project management software.

Up to this point we have only briefly mentioned computers. As you will probably be aware, most project managers today make extensive use of computer software in their project management. Computers are merely a tool to help you do what you want to do;

they depend on the information which you put into them to carry out their tasks.

The computer cannot manage the project for you

The computer cannot manage the project for you. But it can provide more detailed information in a wide variety of formats more quickly than any human can. And it can manipulate the information you put into the system to provide the output in many different forms.

However, it is *essential* that you understand the basic concepts of project management before you attempt to put your project onto a computer system.

There are many off the shelf software packages available and in this chapter we will be considering the use of these. The commissioning of a custom built package is a much more complex subject and would require the input of experienced project management techniques as well as Information Technology skills beyond the scope of this book.

POTENTIAL USES OF COMPUTER SOFTWARE

The charts and networks produced as part of the planning process lend themselves readily to computerization, but to produce the charts you have to put in the basic information.

In Chapters 7 to 9 we looked at the techniques for planning a project and in Chapters 10 to 13 at the importance of monitoring and controlling the project and considered techniques you could use to do this. Once you have entered the basic data into a computer project management package, it will manipulate the data to provide information in many different forms. For these reports to be accurate and up to date you will need not only to plan the project well in the first instance, but also to add updating information as the project progresses. This is not as onerous as it seems and one of the great benefits of computerization is that updating one item will automatically update all others that it affects. In this way you can see what effects any, even minor, changes to plans are having.

PLANNING YOUR PROJECT

You can put the initial planning data into a computer project management package and it will produce for you charts similar to those we looked at in Chapter 6. Examples are shown in Figures 14.1 and 14.2 later in this chapter.

The amount of information the computer will give you will depend on what you put in to start with. In most programs the project can be planned as either resource driven or time driven.

Exactly how you enter the data and manipulate it varies from program to program. We will not go into the details of that here. It is the principles of what these programs can do (and which are all similar) which are of general interest. If you are considering purchasing a package some guidelines are given later in this chapter, and once that decision has been made you should consider undertaking training in the use of that package. A day or two spent doing this will greatly assist you in making the best use of the software.

PLANNING TIME

To plan you project on the computer you will have to list all the activities or tasks, the time required for each (either as overall time or work units) and allocate the resources to each of these activities. You would do this in a similar way to the planning process we described in Chapters 7 and 8. You could do this on paper first, but as you get more familiar with the computer system you will find it easy to enter directly onto the program.

In some packages this can be done only on the Gantt chart, in others you could enter this initial information on either the Gantt chart or the PERT chart. You will decide which you are most comfortable with and be guided by the priorities of your project. Time driven projects can easily be entered via the PERT chart, but resource driven projects are better entered via the Gantt chart.

Some people like to use a combination of these two charts. When you are training to use your software package you will learn the benefits of each.

You can group your activities according to summary headings and produce a simplified chart which contains only the summary information. This is particularly useful in long or complex projects. It can also be a convenient way to show information to managers or clients who do not require the full details of the complete plan.

You can add constraints such as non-working days, certain tasks which must not start before given dates and so on and input these to the system, too. At this initial planning stage you can also add a cost element by putting in information about the charges for various resources.

DEPENDENCIES

When you have listed all the activities and allocated a time to them, you will need to decide which tasks are dependent on which and link them accordingly. This is the way of showing the dependencies which we described in Chapter 7.

Once you have entered the dependencies onto the program with your activities and resources, it can work out information such as earliest and latest start and finish dates for individual activities as well as the complete project.

RESOURCE DRIVEN PROJECTS

These are projects where the resources are fixed. By entering your project plan, with information on the available resources and total work required for each activity, the program will work out the time required for each activity. When the dependencies are added it will give the total project time, earliest and latest starts and finishes.

As before, this requires you to input accurate information at the initial planning stage, but it can save a great deal of time later.

TIME-DRIVEN PROJECT

These are projects where the time required or allowed for activities is the controlling factor. When you plan a project for this priority and enter the time allowed for each activity, the program can work out the resources required.

If you have limited resources you can enter these and the program will work out when resources are over allocated. This means you can easily see where more resources are required to meet the timescales necessary.

THE CRITICAL PATH

When time, work and resources have been entered, the program will automatically work out the critical path of your project. This gives you the ability to alter the parameters (time or resources) to move some items of the critical path and see the effects of your changes very quickly.

'WHAT IF'S' AND PROJECT CHANGES

Save the project for security, then try out 'what if' scenarios which can lead to much more accurate planning

Once you have entered your project you can move and manipulate the data in many different ways. You should first save the project for the sake of security, then you can try out 'what if' scenarios. For example, you can look at the effect of adding more resources, lengthening the time of an activity or altering a dependency. You could look at the results of a delay in certain activities, or of adding additional activities to the project.

For example, if you are running a project which is time critical you can establish which tasks are on the critical path. You can then look at the results of a delay in certain activities. This could help in your planning as you will be able to see if you need to build in contingencies, or allow extra budget to pull in more resources at key times.

Using these 'what if' scenarios can lead to much more accurate planning, as well as saving an enormous amount of time while you are running the project and can help with contingency planning or deciding on changes caused by problems during the progress of the project.

PROJECT PLANS

Figures 14.1 and 14.2 show typical examples of the type of plan a computer program will produce. They are the Gantt chart and PERT chart for the same project. These printouts vary from software to software, but the principal information will be similar.

With many programs you can customize your charts to print out in specific styles to suit your needs.

COSTS

Computer project management programs also have the ability to include cost information. You can enter costs against resources either on a daily or hourly rate or on a 'per use' basis. This information will then be included in the calculations when the time for each resource is allocated and can be updated as the project progresses.

Some programs have the ability to pull in information from other programs, so you could combine a spreadsheet from one program with your project plan on another. This depends on the compatibility of information and if you are likely to require this you should enquire about it when assessing packages for your needs.

OTHER CHARTS AND REPORTS

As well as the Gantt and PERT charts shown in Figures 14.1 and 14.2, computer software can produce other information as project reports. This can take the form of notes to the plan which you have

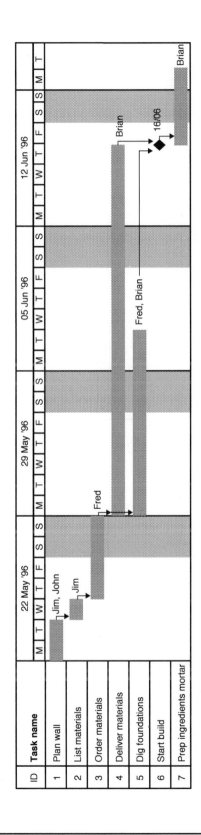

FIGURE 14.1: Computer generated Gantt chart

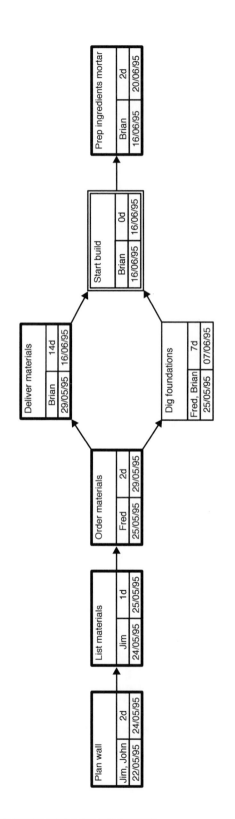

Note: The darker boxes and arrows show the critical path; the double box is a milestone.

FIGURE 14.2: Computer generated PERT chart

typed in yourself, but could also show manpower or resource utilization, work required for specific resources or cost information. All of these are derived automatically from the data you put in at the initial planning stage and the progress information you should enter at regular intervals during the progress of the project.

Some examples of how completed work is shown are given in Figures 14.3 and 14.4.

Different software packages may produce different reports. When selecting a package find out what reports it produces and compare these with a list of your requirements.

SUMMARIZING AND COMBINING PROJECTS

In complex projects with many activities it is often convenient to summarize the activity packages for some purposes, but expand into more details for other requirements. A computer package will normally allow you to do this.

Most packages will allow you to bring together different projects, this is particularly useful where you are sharing one or more resources between projects. By combining the projects into one large one you can easily see where resources are over or under utilized.

MONITORING AND CONTROL

Make your plan control the project by using the computer to update information on a regular basis

Once you have put in all the planning data you can then use your plan to control the project. You will need to monitor the progress whether you are using a computer or not, but with the computer you can update the information on a regular basis and any recalculation of costs and times will be done for you. But you must remember to put in *all* the relevant data or the recalculations will not be accurate.

SELECTING A SOFTWARE PACKAGE

There are so many good packages available on the market now that it is difficult to know how to begin selecting one. You may wish to take the advice of your company systems or IT specialists if these are available. But even if you can call on specialist advice it is worth considering what your needs are first – that way you will not get

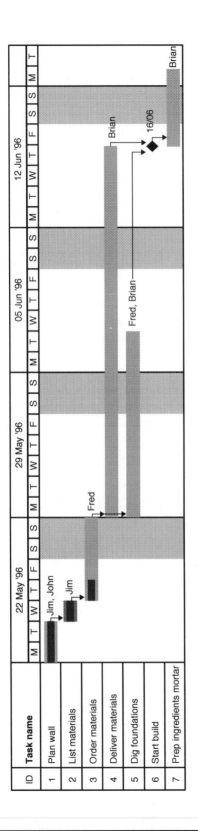

Note: Completed work is shown by a dark line within the bar.

FIGURE 14.3: Gantt chart showing completed work

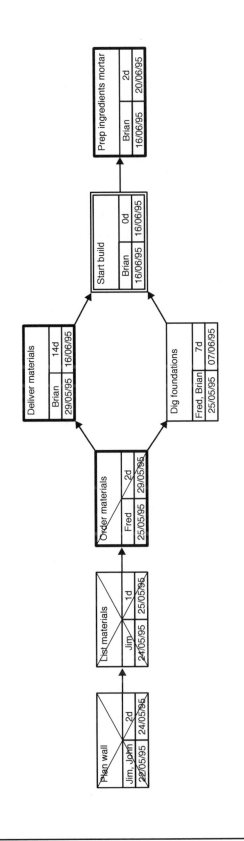

Note: Completed work is shown by the boxes crossed through.

FIGURE 14.4: PERT chart showing completed work

blinded with jargon or talked into buying and using an unsuitable product.

There are various stages which should be considered when selecting a package for use on a particular project or project type. These are listed below:

1. Identify the key requirements
2. Identify any other desirable attributes
3. Consider the likely maximum size of your project
4. Compare your requirements with the package specification
5. Test out a sample project on the 'bestfit' package
6. If everything is satisfactory – purchase the package.

To help you set out your criteria (points 1 and 2 above) I list below a variety of criteria which might be required for a program. It is a starting point for you to check software against, but it is not exhaustive and you may wish to add your own criteria.

CHECKLIST

1. Speed of operation
2. Disk space required and loading medium (disk or CD)
3. Accessibility of all reporting and charting facilities
4. Windows or DOS version required
5. Method of data entry, does it suit your requirements?
6. Ease of editing and updating
7. Ability to handle multiple projects
8. Capability of scheduling common resources across multiple projects
9. What displays and reports will it produce?
10. Quality of the printouts
11. Ability to monitor progress
12. Effectiveness of manual and other documentation
13. Training and support available
14. Overall ease of use
15. Compatibility with other software
16. Upgrades available for future changes and their likely cost.

ESTABLISHING SOFTWARE NEEDS

If you do not already have a software package or are buying one with a particular project in mind, you will need to establish what the exact requirements of the package are for your particular needs. This will help you to identify the most suitable package.

Take into account the abilities and needs of the project and the team

As well as the ability of the package to do what you want, the project manager should also take into account the abilities and needs of the project and the team. For example, who will have to use the package? Are they comfortable with computers? Who will need to interpret the charts and reports? Do they need help in this?

SESSION 14 – EXERCISE WITH YOUR TEAM

OVERVIEW
The purpose of the exercise is to help you establish the criteria for your software needs. If you already have a package you are using and happy with, you may choose to omit this session. If you have a package but are not sure if it is meeting your needs then it will be worthwhile going through this exercise.

EQUIPMENT AND MATERIALS
You will require a flip chart.

PREPARATION
One the left-hand side of your chart, write up a copy of the checklist given in this chapter. Leave the other side blank for comments.

METHOD
Discussion.

TIME
About 20–30 minutes, plus some follow up.

Exercise 14.1

Steps
1. Tell the team that you are considering the software needs of your projects. Decide whether you are going to carry this out with one particular project in mind or consider all the general software needs of the likely projects your team may have to undertake in the foreseeable future.
2. Consider each of the criteria in the checklist. Note of each one:

    – If it is relevant to our projects
    – Exactly what it means to our team's needs.

3. Are there any other criteria to add, if so, note these.
4. Task someone with producing the agreed checklist as a handout for all team members.
5. Ask all team members to go away and collect information on any software packages they know of or can find out about. (The advertisements in *Project* magazine are useful, as will be discussion with other project managers and software users.) Ask them to get as much information as possible to compare with your checklist. Set a date and agree to meet back to share this information.
6. Meet back and share the information. Decide which is the most likely package. Arrange a demonstration of the one or two your think are most likely to be suitable.

SUMMARY

USES OF COMPUTER SOFTWARE

Computers can only help project management when they are given accurate and up to date information. This means that the project manager first needs to know the techniques for good project planning and control without computer assistance.

Once the accurate information is input the computer program can assist the project manager in a number of ways:

■ Producing Gantt or PERT charts from basic data
■ Producing a number of different charts and reports from the same data showing resource allocation and over usage
■ Calculating complex figures quickly and accurately
■ When one item is updated, updating all connected or affected items
■ Trying 'what if' scenarios quickly and simply.

ESTABLISHING SOFTWARE NEEDS

To acquire a program which will work well for you, you will need to establish your needs. This can be done by answering the following questions:

■ What does it cost?
■ What training and ongoing support is available?
■ Can it be updated if a new version is brought out?
■ Is it compatible with any other software we have?

- Has my computer got enough memory to run it?
- Can it handle enough different activities and resources for my needs?
- Can it handle enough different projects for my needs?
- Can it combine projects and resources if required?
- Can the data be entered in the way I prefer?
- Is it logical, user friendly and easy to learn?
- Can the project be edited and updated easily?
- Does it produce all the reports I need?
- Can it use existing printers or will I need a new one?
- What is the quality of the printouts?

*F*URTHER USEFUL INFORMATION

The Association for Project Management
85 Oxford Road
High Wycombe
Buckinghamshire HP11 2DX
United Kingdom
Tel: 01494 400900

Internet
(*NB* This is the name of an organization, not the international computer communications system)

The International Project Management Association
Zurich
Switzerland

INDEX